A New Approach to Cross-Cultural People Management

When managing cross-culturally in a polarized world, recognizing similarities between people and establishing common ground can be key to success. This book argues that despite differences in language, political systems, income levels, and other factors, people are people.

There is no doubt that cultural differences should be understood and appreciated, not only because this is the right thing to do in a multicultural world, but because failure to understand these differences when doing business can result in costly mistakes. But when managing people, what matters most is showing respect and interest – because what motivates (and de-motivates) is the same regardless of cultural background. This book explains and illustrates eight themes in which people are very similar across cultures, including trust, fairness, integrity, and, though often overlooked in an organizational context, the reasons why people work.

Business leaders, human resource professionals, organizational consultants, and students in these fields will appreciate this fresh perspective on people management, and the mini-cases and interviews with senior executives provide inspiring real-world examples.

Robert Grosse is Professor of International Business and Director for Latin America at Thunderbird School of Global Management at Arizona State University in Phoenix, Arizona. He joined Thunderbird in August 1994, and rejoined in 2016. He was Director of Leadership Development at Standard Bank in South Africa during 2006–9, Dean of the graduate business school, EGADE, at Monterrey Tec in Mexico after that, and then Dean of the business school at American University of Sharjah in the UAE before returning to Thunderbird. He holds a B.A. degree from Princeton University and a Ph.D. from the University of North Carolina, both in international economics. He has taught international finance and global strategy as a full-time faculty member in the MBA programs at Thunderbird, the University of Miami, the University of Michigan, and at the Instituto de Empresa (Madrid, Spain). He has also taught in many universities throughout Latin America. Professor Grosse is a Fellow of the Academy of International Business and of the Business Association for Latin American Studies. He was President of the Business Association of Latin American Studies in 2005–6 and President of the Academy of International Business during 2012–14.

A New Approach to Cross-Cultural People Management

People are People

Robert Grosse

Routledge
Taylor & Francis Group

NEW YORK AND LONDON

Designed cover image: © Getty Images

First published 2023
by Routledge
605 Third Avenue, New York, NY 10158

and by Routledge
4 Park Square, Milton Park, Abingdon, Oxon, OX14 4RN

Routledge is an imprint of the Taylor & Francis Group, an informa business

Library of Congress Cataloging-in-Publication Data
Names: Grosse, Robert E., author.
Title: A new approach to cross-cultural people management :
people are people / Robert Grosse.
Description: New York, NY : Routledge, 2023. |
Includes bibliographical references and index.
Identifiers: LCCN 2022050403 (print) | LCCN 2022050404 (ebook) |
ISBN 9781032434797 (hardback) | ISBN 9781032434780 (paperback) |
ISBN 9781003367512 (ebook)
Subjects: LCSH: Diversity in the workplace–Management. |
Multiculturalism. | Personnel management. | International business
enterprises–Personnel management.
Classification: LCC HF5549.5.M5 G76 2023 (print) |
LCC HF5549.5.M5 (ebook) | DDC 658.3/008–dc23/eng/20221020
LC record available at https://lccn.loc.gov/2022050403
LC ebook record available at https://lccn.loc.gov/2022050404

ISBN: 9781032434797 (hbk)
ISBN: 9781032434780 (pbk)
ISBN: 9781003367512 (ebk)

DOI: 10.4324/9781003367512

Typeset in Bembo
by Newgen Publishing UK

Contents

Chapter 1

People really are people

People are people. There is no difference between people from Japan and people from Canada, other than skin color, language and some of their cultural practices. Of course, individuals are different from each other, and every human being is unique. But there is no need for you or me to understand some kind of alien being in order to know what makes our neighbor tick. Anybody is happy to be praised for doing something good or doing something well. Anybody is sad to have their failings criticized. Maybe a Latin American person would prefer to be less direct in discussing personal or organizational issues than a 'typical' US person. Maybe an Asian person would likewise be less likely to confront a problem with a co-worker or boss rather than try to work around it, in contrast with a German person. But at the end of the day we are all humans, and the desire for positive reinforcement of our actions is common to all of us.

Consider how different people are in Japan, where they bow to each other in greeting, to France where they kiss each other on both cheeks, to India where they place their hands in a praying position toward each other, to the United States where people shake hands – the greeting procedures are quite strikingly different. This difference was blurred greatly during the Covid-19 pandemic, when people largely did not touch each other with their greetings, and so greetings were much more similar. Once the pandemic retreated in 2021, the greeting practices began returning to the pre-pandemic styles – although some degree of separation remained common in the first half of 2022. People, or rather practices, are very different across cultures. At the same time, when a boss tells a subordinate that he/she did a good job on some task, the subordinate will be happy and feel good, possibly for a long time. This is true in China, Germany, Australia, Argentina and everywhere in between. People in this context of being congratulated or thanked are very much the same across countries. So, how do we reconcile these two almost polar opposite points of view?

At the end of the day, around the world people are people. They are motivated by the same desires, de-motivated by the same negative factors

DOI: 10.4324/9781003367512-1

and generally much more similar than different. It is valuable to understand this fundamental principle, and then to see what works in dealing with people everywhere. This is particularly important in a business context, where executives and managers have to deal with subordinates, peers, bosses and outsiders such as customers and suppliers. It is useful as well to consider some of the many slight differences that produce results that in fact are different between cultures. For example, everybody wants food to eat, housing to living in and a job to provide income to the family. Everybody would like a secure, nonthreatening environment to live in and other (government-assured) protections. But not everybody places the same priorities among these goals, and for example the Chinese expect very different support from their government than people in the United States expect from theirs. But still, everybody likes praise for their work, and nobody likes criticism, even if deserved.

The goal of this book is to demonstrate how very similar people are around the world, despite cultural traditions and practices that sometimes vary widely. If you want to convey gratitude to someone, you don't need to know much about cultural differences – you just need to get out there and say it! If you want to demonstrate that you treat people fairly, you don't need a detailed cultural analysis on how to express this quality – you just need to show it. Once you understand these similarities among people, the book presents a range of methods for using these similarities to get the most out of your organization's people and to deal most successfully with people in other organizations such as those of your customers and suppliers.

This is a cross-cultural(!), people management book. Rather than focusing on differences between people from different countries, it focuses on the many, many similarities of people across all countries. Rather than emphasizing different corporate cultures or differences between people in different organizations, the discussion focuses on what is the same in any organization comprised of people. And finally, it considers what a manager or an executive can do to achieve the organization's goals first by understanding these elements along which people are the same and then utilizing this knowledge to manage more successfully.

As you will see in the discussion later, much of the contrast between the emphasis on *differences* between people and the emphasis on *similarities* between people comes from two very different approaches. Sociology or cultural anthropology looks at the differences between people based on cultural conditions. These may range from language to level of economic development to religion to tribal or clan practices or yet other dimensions. Psychology looks at characteristics of people as human beings – and these are much more similar around the world than different. People have basic needs and wants, and they respond to stimuli in similar manners. So, the discussion here emphasizes the psychology perspective rather than the sociology one – although both are relevant to our understanding of how to deal with people.

When it comes to managing people in an organization, or dealing with people in a business context more broadly, there are numerous elements that operate similarly across cultures and around the world. Managing people works best if people feel committed to the organization. This can come from a variety of factors, but one important factor is the way that the boss treats people in the organization. Being unethical or biased in the way that you deal with people is not accepted in any culture, even though people may make less of an explicit statement of disagreement in different cultures. If the boss regularly lies to the employees, this behavior will be rejected by those employees in one way or another, and that boss is likely to be forced out, since the behavior hurts the organization. If the boss shows even-handed treatment of people in the organization, this behavior will be both accepted and rewarded with more loyal and committed employees.

One key takeaway from this book will be a set of guidelines for dealing with people, based on different situations/contexts/elements/drivers. The main ones discussed in the chapters below are:

1   What *motivates* people across cultures?
    a   How do people react to *praise or thanks* (for doing a good job)?
        i   How should you give praise or thanks to them?
    b   What other factors help to motivate members of the organization?
        i   These include things ranging from opportunities for self-realization to higher salaries/bonuses
2   What *de-motivates* people across cultures?
    a   How do people react to *criticism* for making mistakes or for doing a bad job?
        i   How should you deliver the negative news to them?
    b   What other factors de-motivate the people in an organization?
        i   These include aspects of the work environment, from bullying or just incompetent managers to high uncertainty about job security and about goals of the company
3   How do you create *trust* between two people from the same or different cultures, and also trust in the organization?
    a   What mechanisms can be used, from demonstrating your own trustworthiness to giving people the opportunity to demonstrate theirs
    b   Being honest and transparent in decision-making can go a long way to establishing trust in the organization
4   How important is it to show *respect* for people in an organization?
    a   How do you measure respect in the first place? Is it respect for people as human beings (owed respect), or for their performance

(earned respect), or for being in a higher position (respect for position)?

   b   How important is self-respect in an organization?

5   How do you demonstrate *fairness* in the way you deal with people?

   a   Fairness can be judged in several ways

       i   Fairness in the process of decision-making

       ii   Fairness in the outcomes of decisions such as hire/fire or salary reviews

       iii   Fairness in identifying the goals of the organization, so that people's work can be aligned with those goals

6   Do people see *honesty/integrity* the same across cultures, or are there differences?

   a   Honesty means telling the truth, while integrity means acting according to acceptable moral principles.

   b   You want people to be honest with each other in the organization, but more importantly you want leaders to act with integrity and set good role models for employees

7   Is being *forward-looking* or *planning ahead* important in a culture or not?

   a   The specific ways in which people are forward-looking may differ across cultures, but companies must look ahead in order to compete successfully

   b   Planning is a mechanism for forcing the organization to look ahead, although it does not create an un-adjustable plan, because conditions do change unexpectedly, and adjustments sometimes have to be made

8   *Why do people work?* Is it just because of the need to have income to support a family's needs, or are there additional reasons? Of course, there are several basic reasons for working, which include:

   a   Earning an income that satisfies the individual

   b   To develop competencies in doing the work required and in building a career and learning new skills

   c   To operate with some degree of autonomy, i.e., to feel that you have some control over your work life

   d   To relate to other people, and to feel that you are part of an organization that is bigger than yourself. This also implies that people seek purpose in their work.

Consider each of these issues in turn.

What motivates people across cultures?

There are certainly many things that motivate people to take actions, to work hard(er) and to pursue other goals. Within an organization motivation is generally seen as that which generates a positive contribution by employees to the organization's goals. That is, motivation pushes people to be more productive or to be more committed to the organization or just to work harder than they otherwise would. So, sources of motivation would be things such as money (salary or wages), status (job level or title), perks (e.g., nice office, good parking place) and even praise or gratitude expressed by the boss.

It is certain that different people are more or less motivated by the same factors. Someone who is toward the lower end of the income distribution is likely to be more motivated by financial rewards, whereas someone who is toward the higher end of incomes is likely to be more motivated by perks or by demonstrations of appreciation for his/her work by the boss. Someone from a collectivist culture may have more motivation from feeling like a part of the group, whereas someone from an individualist culture may gain more motivation from distinguishing him/herself from the pack. Regardless of the context, everyone is motivated by some positive factor(s) that will spur them on to superior performance – and it is up to the leader to figure out which factors they are.

What de-motivates people across cultures?

Just as there are factors that motivate people to contribute more to an organization's success, there are factors that de-motivate them as well. A feeling that one's work is not appreciated probably ranks high among negative factors in the workplace. Likewise, a sense of unfair treatment within the organization is likely to be a disincentive to work there. A clear demotivator is to criticize someone in front of co-workers. This behavior is almost always harmful, since it both demotivates the person, and by humiliating him/her, it sends a negative message to the whole team.

Annual performance reviews in many organizations, especially in large ones, are common practice. There are always likely to be some negative issues raised for anyone, if only because the boss feels compelled to say something critical (or suggesting improvement) just to balance out positive comments. The challenge is to make the comments aiming for improvement in a manner that produces a desire by the employee to try to do better, rather than to feel oppressed by recognition of weaknesses.

Negative feedback often demotivates people for sure. In addition, a difficult work environment that is noisy, crowded, isolated or having some other feature that the employee dislikes raise another challenge to encouraging people. In this instance, it may not be a direct negative comment to the employee, but an environment that is simply de-motivating. The boss can probably resolve this kind of problem fairly readily – if it is recognized. This is another feature of dealing with people that is challenging: How can you recognize when someone is feeling oppressed or let down by the organization?

How do you create trust between two people from the same or different cultures?

This may seem like a simple task. You just allow people to interact within the team/organization, and over time they will develop trust in each other. This definitely does not always happen, and it may take a long time for trust to develop if it ever does. The challenge for the boss is to identify methods of obtaining trust from co-workers, whether by demonstrated behavior or by some other means. A possible step is to explicitly state that you will trust people in the organization unless they demonstrate untrustworthy behavior. This may be a good starting point in some cultures, but in others it is an affront to even mention the issue. At the end of the day it is most likely that trust will be developed from demonstrated behavior.

It may be possible to generate trust by offering an employee the opportunity to work without supervision. This is certainly an issue that appeared frequently during the Covid-19 pandemic, with many people working (more or less unsupervised) from home. By force rather than by choice bosses were led to give greater autonomy to people working at a distance. A resulting challenge from this situation was that it was difficult to give people a sense of belonging to the organization when they were working from home – and perhaps continuing to do so.

How important is it to show respect for people in different cultures?

What does it mean to show respect? Is it the idea of bowing to an elderly person, in the Oriental style of demonstrating respect for age? Does it mean to give equal voice to people on a team at work? There is really no one manner of showing respect, but the issue is very important to the cohesiveness of a team.

For example, showing that you respect someone can generate a high degree of commitment from the recipient of this treatment. And likewise showing a lack of respect or lack of valuing a person's contribution can lead to a great degree of alienation or de-motivation of the person – so this should be avoided. How can you show respect? This is as simple as including people in meetings, calling on them to contribute to discussions, and generally making them feel wanted in the team/organization. It means not criticizing a person's contribution to the discussion, even if it appears not to be useful at the time. This last point is a major one, because it is often difficult not to react negatively to what is perceived to be an off-base or trivial contribution by a team member. On the other hand, anyone with managerial experience realizes that sometimes a contribution may not appear useful at the time or in the context – but later it may prove very valuable indeed. For example, someone at Apple criticizing Steve Jobs' argument that the company should get into the business of making cell phones would have been very appropriate before the iPhone. With hindsight we can see that it was brilliant idea.

Respect is as simple as recognizing the value of another person. This may be in terms of the person's technical skill or knowledge, or in terms of their ability to explain things well, or even the ability to bring a group of people together in discussing an issue.

A really confounding aspect of respect is that it has to exist in the eyes of the person receiving that respect. You can make as much of an effort as you think appropriate to convey this feeling to someone, but unless their perception is in line with your effort, the respect may not be there. I worked with many women at the bank in South Africa, and I found frequently that unless I explicitly stated how much I valued their views, there was a sense of resistance or discontent from that person. Because the organization was not populated by many women in high positions, those who were in managerial or executive roles often felt marginalized unless they were encouraged to participate in decision-making and to offer their opinions.

How do you demonstrate fairness in the way you deal with people?

Just as with respect, fairness is in the eye of the person receiving the treatment. The boss or the person trying to demonstrate fair behavior will not have succeeded if the employee or other person does not perceive the treatment as being fair. This is a fascinating challenge, because even if a decision-maker uses completely neutral criteria, the perception may still not be that a decision is fair. Think about admissions criteria to US universities, where the universities try to seek ethnic balance in their admitted students, but Chinese and Indian students claim discrimination because they are not admitted in proportion to their comparatively higher entrance exam scores (SAT, ACT), and white students complain that they are not fairly treated relative to black students, because of university efforts to increase the percentage of black students.

Fairness at the bank in South Africa definitely called for disproportionate selection and promotion of non-white employees at all levels, consistent with the fact that about 90% of South Africans are black or colored, while whites had better business experience because the whites were favored under the Apartheid system up until 1994.

Thus, the way in which fairness is interpreted depends on the context, but it always reflects the recipient's feeling of being included or left out.

Do people see honesty/integrity the same across cultures, or are there differences?

One of the most important traits of a good leader worldwide has been identified as integrity. A person whose word you can trust is someone with integrity. This trait must be demonstrated by actions rather than words. I don't know about you, but if someone says 'trust me' to me, I immediately don't believe what they are saying. Trust comes from hearing the person say that he is going to do X, and then they follow up by doing it. Or when a person says that she will recommend you for a promotion or for an opportunity at work – and then she does it. The action is typically not difficult or complicated, but trust does not develop until the act is completed.

This idea is really interesting in a cultural sense, because we often talk about some countries being subject to greater or lesser degrees of corruption in business. If we think of corruption as being a kind of dishonest behavior, then the problem is more severe in countries such as Venezuela, Somalia or North Korea. And at the other extreme, we find the least corrupt countries to be in Scandinavia and New Zealand (based on Transparency International's annual survey). There are certainly trustworthy, honest people in any country, but the prevalence of corruption in some places means that trustworthy behavior is harder to find.

Maybe there is a difference in how dishonest behavior is perceived in different countries. Having lived in six countries, from the United States, Canada and Spain to South Africa, Peru and the United Arab Emirates, I cannot say that dishonesty is more acceptable in one place than another. It is true that one society may demonstrate a willingness to let people evade taxes more than another country. So, the definition of dishonesty probably has to be limited somewhat. Dishonesty in dealing with co-workers in an organization is fairly well understood and considered undesirable behavior everywhere. But at the same time, paying off an official to get the paperwork completed for buying your house or getting goods through customs or for some other bureaucratic issue that is not resolved quickly is hard to criticize. After all, Americans commonly will slip a waiter or maître d' $20 to get a table quicker in a restaurant than what the waiting line offers.

Is being forward-looking or planning ahead important in a culture or not?

The issues up to this point have been presented to demonstrate common behaviors and perceptions of people around the world. Even so, some differences across cultures or countries have been noted. What about forward-looking behavior? This is a fascinating concept to explore, since Western people tend to see this trait as desirable and important, while some other cultures are less forward-looking. Mansour Javidan et al. (2007) found that people from Singapore and Scandinavia plus the United States and Canada were more forward-looking than in other countries, while in Argentina, Russia, Poland and Hungary they focused more on the present.

For organizations a process of strategic planning can be very valuable in helping people to think about the future and about the company's strategy.

The future cannot be known, but the effort to think about it in a structured way, and to consider possible ways to deal with future challenges such as competition, regulation, technology change can help leaders of the firm to design responses to those challenges. This does not differ across cultures, even though the way the process works may very well differ.

Ultimately, what we would like to know is whether or not a forward-looking behavior helps the company perform better, or if having a strategic plan enables the company to make better decisions. If forward-looking behavior is something that an organization wants to foster among its employees, then there had better be a connection from that behavior to the company's performance.

What are the reasons that people work?

Fulfilling basic needs is surely a concern in any society, but even in poor countries people work to achieve not just income for survival but also to fit into an organization or group of people and to learn how to do a better job. If a person is living at a subsistence level of existence, then that person will have a very different priority list than someone who is a millionaire in the United States today. Both people will need food, clothing and shelter – but the first person in the subsistence environment will clearly need to focus first on obtaining the necessities for survival before worrying about leisure activities or discretionary purchases. The second person will probably be more like you and me, and will not be completely absorbed by making ends meet, leaving some opportunity for education, entertainment and other activities. However, even in poor societies, most people live beyond the subsistence level, and so the additional concerns of learning skills, fitting into and rising up in an organization, and feeling contentment from the work environment are also relevant.

There are many conceptual approaches to identifying why people work, and the discussion in this chapter is organized along the lines of Deci and Ryan (e.g., 2015). They talk about three kinds of factor that motivate people to work. First is to achieve competence at your work, which may produce praise from superiors and also financial and promotion rewards. Second is to have some degree of autonomy in your work, so that you can feel some sense of ability to control your (work) life and not be completely bound by rules and oversight. And third is to relate to other people, for both social/human interaction and also to feel a sense of purpose in your work. There are several other approaches to organizing our thinking about why people work, such as Herzberg et al.'s (1959) categories of hygiene and motivation, and McClelland's (1961) theory based on three factors: achievement, affiliation and power. The additional conceptual approaches tend to go further in systematically identifying the motivations for work beyond subsistence income, and we will limit the discussion here to one approach.

In this chapter on reasons for working, and also earlier in the book, we look at how the Covid-19 pandemic has affected people's work lives and their attitudes toward work. Many things have changed since the onset of the pandemic in 2020, but the issues raised in the chapters have not changed. Perhaps the fact that the United States achieved very low unemployment levels in the past decade, less than 4% except in the 2020–21 height of the pandemic, means that people see more opportunities to work today, and thus more freedom to look for job attributes beyond income. The idea that Millennials may see things differently from their predecessors in the Baby Boom and Generations X and Y is also considered. In fact, the work environment is changing very significantly, with more work from home or away from the office, more flexible work hours, and more use of electronic means to communicate and keep records. These changes along with the generational change make understanding work today quite a challenge – which this book explores through both the analytical approach used and with many quotes from business leaders about their experiences.

In fact, throughout the book there are statements from business leaders in industries from manufacturing to services to mining and oil, presenting their views on each of the issues raised in the chapters. They talk about motivating people in their organizations from South Africa to the United States, from Peru to the United Kingdom, and in China and India among the various countries included. There was no single view offered by these businesspeople with decades of experience in managing and leading people – but all of them recognized common threads such as how people react to praise and criticism, and how important non-income aspects are in creating a positive work environment.

A couple of the many businesspeople interviewed for this project were quite adamant about recognizing differences in people they have managed in different countries, and less enthusiastic about recognizing the common features of people across countries and cultures. This resistance is expected among academics as well, since many business writers tend to focus on cultural differences and very few look at commonalties as we do here. One may choose his/her focus on issues of people's behavior, but I don't think that anyone can contradict the fundamental premise here: People Are People.

Conclusions

The different elements discussed above provide the context for the next chapters. We will proceed to look first at the things that motivate people. Second, we will look at things that do the opposite, that is, things that de-motivate people. These two elements will make you realize that people really are people in having similar reactions to situations of these two elements. The rest of the book then digs into the additional kinds of items that characterize human beings the world over. By the end you will recognize that people really are people, and that our differences in language, culture and other features do not change this fundamental reality.

References

Deci, Edward, and Richard Ryan, 2015. Self-Determination Theory. *International Encyclopedia of the Social & Behavioral Sciences*, 2nd ed., Volume 21, 487–91. Amsterdam: Elsevier.

Herzberg, Frederick, Bernard Mausner, and Barbara Bloch, Snyderman, 1959. *The Motivation to Work*, 2nd ed. New York: John Wiley.

Javidan, Mansour, Richard M. Steers, and Michael A. Hitt, 2007. *The Global Mindset* (Advances in International Management, Vol. 19). Bingley: Emerald Group Publishing.

McClelland, David, 1961. *The Achieving Society*. Princeton, NJ: Van Nostrand.

Chapter 2

What motivates people?

What can motivate a person or a team in your organization to pursue an unreachable goal, or at least one that seems unreachable on the face of it? How do you get people to put their minds and efforts into figuring out how to build a better mousetrap – or a more elegant computer program or an autonomous vehicle or a new clothing fabric? And for services, how can you motivate people to provide better service to their customers in a grocery store, or to their online customers in a bank, or to their users of a platform on the internet for purchasing products?

Encouraging people does not have to mean getting them to be innovators, although that is often desirable, but rather it means providing them with a positive environment and personal feedback that demonstrates that you care about them and their work. While money/compensation is certainly one form of demonstrating that you think that a person is doing a good and valuable job, there are also many other tools for motivating people, a number of which work better than money. Herzberg (2003) for example, focuses on *intrinsic* rewards such as offering people interesting, challenging work and the opportunity to progress in their careers. He and others find that money is definitely a secondary consideration for motivating people in an organization, while "motivation is founded upon satisfaction born of a sense of achievement, recognition for achievement, responsibility and personal growth" (Bassett-Jones and Lloyd 2005).

This theme is what launched me into writing the current book, since I found that motivating people is so similar across countries and cultures. While there are many ways to motivate people in organizations and in general, the one most striking way is to offer positive feedback. That is, praise for doing a good job, thanks for helping to accomplish a goal, or just a kind word to demonstrate that you appreciate what the person is doing. Every one of the executives that I talked with about this project made the same kind of statement: authentic praise for doing a good job goes a very long way in motivating people. Still, praise just like money is not the only factor that will get people to feel committed to working for an organization or to

DOI: 10.4324/9781003367512-2

be more productive. This chapter looks at half a dozen of these factors, and explores how and why they work.

Praise

The number one answer to motivating people is surely: praise them. The more you tell people that you appreciate their efforts and encourage them to keep going, the more likely that they will. Just think of your own experience when a boss or a teacher or a coach told you that you were doing a great job, and that he/she really appreciated it. The praise makes you feel happy, and makes you want to do more that will lead to more praise. Of course, the praise has to be authentic, and you really do have to feel that the person is doing a good job and that you want to recognize that fact with your praise. Superficial statements of thanks or congratulations will be recognized as just that, and they will fail.

A senior executive in a consumer products company said:

> When I was in Geneva, Switzerland, this was the first performance review of my assistant brand manager who joined the company a year prior. He was a young French man fresh out of college. As we started the review, I talked about how much of a good job he has done adapting to his new role over the past year. I conveyed my observation and appreciation for his eagerness to learn and the effort he puts in to deliver on his projects. We talked about a couple of specific deliverables where he truly shined. His face lit up and there was a smile on his face that lasted throughout the review even when we were talking about some of the areas for improvement for the upcoming year. He was very open to receiving constructive criticism and even suggested a few ideas that he thought may help him grow in his role.

The message from this statement is twofold: first, the praise for good work was gratefully received. And second, by pointing out weaknesses in the same discussion as providing the praise, this executive was able to avoid de-motivating the subordinate due to the feedback about weaknesses.

As a manager/executive, I found this one thing to be the best motivator of people who worked for me in banking, in universities, in government and in consulting. Telling someone that you value their contribution is truly an amazing motivator. And the means of getting this message across can either be praise for the work being done or thanks for the person's commitment to get the job done. Depending on the context, one or the other of these demonstrations of appreciation may produce better results. The idea of praising a person means that the person will recognize that the boss understands the contribution being made. The idea of thanking someone for their work means that the boss is demonstrating his/her appreciation of what the person is doing. These are not identical ideas, and the boss may use both motivators together, or just one of them, as the circumstances dictate.

There are certainly differences in how you might approach this subject of giving praise or thanks in different cultures. For example, when I worked in the United Arab Emirates (UAE), I found a huge gap in expectations between local nationals (Emiratis) and foreign nationals who make up 90% of the UAE population. Emiratis since the discovery of oil and gas in the country in the early 1970s have lived a sheltered life, with most things such as education, housing and health care given to them as a birthright. This is a feasible policy when the annual per capita income in 2019 was about $US 70,000. The 'guest workers' from other countries, from maids and taxi drivers to petroleum engineers and physicians, receive salaries or wages as in most countries. The contrast is huge, but the response to praise was pretty uniformly very positive and long-lasting from both groups of people. The Emiratis expect to have many things given to them, and they often have servants to provide food service and other help at home. Even so, they respond positively to praise.

Local people in this unusual situation were clearly motivated by praise from their boss or teacher, although some amount of praise was expected regardless of performance – so the challenge is to offer meaningful praise. In this atypical context, the Emiratis for instance were very much motivated when their manager or boss made statements to thank them for their work or just for their efforts. Because the local people have so little need to work due to the oil wealth, the general level of motivation for them is quite low. When someone such as the boss says honestly that he appreciates what they are doing, this personal touch makes a huge difference.

A senior university executive and former university president, working in the UAE for a decade said that:

> I typically do not miss a day without saying something positive to everyone with whom I have contact. This may be considered a weakness in management, but for me, there is an element of the Machiavellian in being positive toward one's direct reports and peers. For one thing, they soon learn to understand the nuance of my positive comments about them. Truly outstanding behavior gets a turbocharged, public display of my approval. Anything less is by contrast lacking in luster, but still positive. Criticisms, in contrast, become less devastating. My rule of thumb is to praise seven times more often than to criticize, a ratio that I read somewhere; it is not original with me. Any senior officer who is stingy with praise will lose loyalty in the long run.

I believe that he used this same approach, with similarly positive results, when leading universities in the United States.

In Monterrey, Mexico, the environment is quite different, even with a major oil industry producing petroleum and natural gas there as well. The population is largely Mexican rather than foreign guest workers, and the family incomes are much lower than in the UAE. However, people had the same response to recognition of the value of their work. Telling a manager in your company that you appreciate her work led to smiles and a sense of fulfillment and an evident willingness to work hard toward the organization's goals. Telling a university administrator that you found his work in dealing with a group of students or creating a report on the success of a new program to be very good just turned on a light in their eyes. It seemed to take days for that glow to wear off, and through that time the person demonstrated a clear enthusiasm for the work.

Another senior executive in a different consumer products company related this story.

> Giving praise with authentic content and style works in every culture, some show more positive emotions in the beginning, some not as much, but at the end it is about the long-term impact. They want to continue creating an impact, learn more and take more responsibility. Currently I work with young graduates in Pakistan, they are eager to learn and have a role model. Positive and constructive feedback helps them for sure. In case of positive feedback, their engagement improves significantly. Organizing a major meeting recently was a big deal for them, and the marketing team did a great job. Thanking them gives them a lot of confidence and [creates an] openness to learn and take on further challenges.

This works for teachers as well as managers. If a teacher tells a student that the student is doing a great job, it will encourage the student to put in even more effort to be praised again. This is not just in the context of grading papers, when a teacher may write a positive comment and give a good grade. This reinforcement certainly is supportive. But even more compelling is if the teacher tells the student that he/she is doing a great job. This verbal praise is more effective than written comments. People respond more fully to the human interaction that a spoken word involves. This is not to say that writing positive comments is not important, but that verbal comments are even more effective.

A senior executive at a major wealth management company, said that his direct reports value greatly the recognition that they are doing a good job. He has observed this behavior in the United States and Latin America where he oversaw managers and salespeople, as well as in the United Kingdom and Europe where he managed a division responsible for private market investment products. He pointed out that "In the highly competitive war to retain top talent, the top performers deeply value recognition, visibility and opportunities to take on stretch assignments. Money matters but recognition broadly speaking is key to creating long term loyalty".

Money/compensation

There is no doubt that compensation for work is important. In the first instance, a person needs income to feed his/her family and pay the bills. Even so, once the basic needs have been covered, financial compensation also rewards a person with the ability to buy other discretionary goods and services. And it may offer a sense of satisfaction to know that the person's compensation is higher than other people's or high relative to a national average or that it is good by some other measure.

Very few people want to be observed as trying to 'keep up with the Joneses', that is, have just as nice a house and car as the people next door. Aiming for this goal is widely perceived as being misguided. But even so, people do observe what their neighbors and colleagues are doing and what things they consume – so peer pressure is very real. As an employer, you want to offer your team members fair and adequate compensation that will enable them to buy things and enjoy themselves with their earnings. How much is enough? There is probably never enough in an ultimate sense, but most people would see compensation that puts them in a financial position similar to that of other people in similar jobs as enough. In other words, they do want to keep up with the Joneses!

I found that even small amounts of compensation can be viewed as very important to people. In my job in the UAE, I gave a direct report a raise of 5% in an annual review. She was very unhappy about this, because one other colleague in a different department received a 5.5% performance-based raise that year. I think that this may have been my biggest mistake in the years I worked there, because this person was so disappointed in receiving only the second highest raise of anyone in the division for her work which was truly outstanding. Despite my verbal thanks to her and praise for the accomplishments that year, it did not overcome the disappointment for failing to be number one. I was quite surprised at the reaction, and after the fact I can see that I should have given a top raise to this person. But the amount of money was small! The key was the relative performance evaluation, and it just seemed like a small issue to me. But people do have different reactions to different aspects of the thanks/praise/reward that they receive in their jobs, and you have to be very attentive to what matters to a particular person.

Sense of purpose

Another aspect of motivation is to give a person a sense of purpose in the work being done. If the person feels that the project or the task has some kind of inherent value, this will encourage him to put in greater effort than if the activity is just a rote repetition. Cutting a lawn on a lawnmower is a pretty routine activity – except that every lawn is different, and there are ways to make the work faster, more efficient and even to produce more esthetic results. A lawn mowing job can give the person a sense of creating beautiful gardens or eye-catching manicured lawns. A bank teller/customer service person can deal with people on the phone such that the client feels a sense of commitment from the bank and also a sense that the service provider is actually paying attention to the client's needs. And if the client reflects this positive interest back to the bank representative, it can give the banker a sense of value in what she is doing.

This sense of purpose is separate from the financial benefits of a job. A particular job may pay well, but it may not make the employee feel like any real value is being produced. An accountant or bookkeeper may put together a financial statement for a client by just adding up receipts for expenses and invoices for sales. This is not particularly challenging or rewarding in the sense of making the accountant feel that the job is important. However, if the accountant can see the recordkeeping work as something that is greatly valued by the client (and if the boss encourages the accountant by stating that the work is valued), then this may produce a feeling of purpose.

The senior executive at the wealth management company, said that most people care deeply about having clear and meaningful feedback from their boss, and having a strong sense of purpose; that what they do matters beyond the bottom line of their company. Fundamentally, they want to understand how their own role is connected to that mission, and also they want to know that somebody (higher up in the organization) cares about it. This is what motivates them, more so than money. On a related note, people also want to achieve a sense of mastery over their work, that shows them and their bosses that they are doing something well, and that it is something that is valued.

This sense is important in any job context. If you are a professional baseball player, and your team performs consistently poorly over several years, it may be difficult to stay motivated. Of course, there is the financial remuneration for a professional athlete, and this generally tends to be quite high. However, being part of a losing team is demoralizing, and it is difficult to see how to deal with such a situation. The ballplayer can focus on his own performance, and seek to be an All-Star or to win a batting title or a Golden Glove award. This is definitely one direction that can work to keep the ballplayer committed and motivated. Another direction is to look for ways to improve the overall team performance, by encouraging teammates, by trying to figure out how the team could perform better (presumably this is the role of the manager, but a player can try to contribute to this group goal as well). This can potentially lead to better performance by the team, but at a minimum it will lead to motivation of the player, who feels like he is doing something worthwhile.

How about an Amazon warehouse worker? This is the kind of job that is regularly reported to be underpaid, very physically demanding and subject to very high turnover. Perhaps Amazon should pay more attention to retaining these workers, but regardless the individuals can be motivated by their own success in meeting productivity goals. Or they can be motivated by working with colleagues who are enjoyable to be around and who make the work experience a positive one. This statement is not to defend or criticize Amazon's practices, but rather to point out that even in an intense workplace, individuals can find satisfaction and motivation from their work.

Recognition

People generally like to be recognized for their positive contributions to the organization or to a project or even to co-workers. While the idea of praise for good work was discussed above, recognition goes beyond the immediate boss or the person who praises another. Recognition implies that more people become aware of the contribution, as when a prize or bonus is awarded to someone for their work. An Employee of the Month award that is posted in the organization, with the winner's picture on it, can be a very motivating kind of recognition.

The idea is that recognition is shared beyond just the boss and the subordinate, or between a division head and a staff person. Recognition is shared with all people in the organization or in the division. Not everybody may pay attention to the award, but it is publicly visible and has an impact on the recipient that can be highly motivating.

In a university, the school (of business) can publicize the articles accepted for publication by professors in the school. This simple recognition can go a long way to motivate many professors to try to publish their work and be seen by their colleagues as succeeding in this way.

The university executive said that, in addition to praise for good work,

> Recognition is key. For faculty, conference attendance and travel are nearly as important as salary and benefits, and research funding from institutional resources on top of conference attendance – plus a press release trumpeting the successful presentation of a conference paper – is icing on the cake. Nearly as important is transparency in the awarding of praise and support of travel for research purposes.

An executive in a construction equipment manufacturing company said that: "Leadership motivates people; our CEO says that people don't work for him, rather they work for the company. He knows most people's first names & background, even with 2000 employees". The evidence that this approach to people works is that the company has a less than 2% annual turnover rate, which is extremely low for the industry.

Job stability

Another motivating factor is job stability. This is one motivation often used to explain why people seek jobs in government. Salaries and wages in government jobs tend not to be high relative to those in the private sector. However, the job security tends to be very high in government (except for elected officials, who serve for predetermined terms of office). Actually, this might not be a good example of motivation, because the job security easily may lead to slacking off on the job, since quality control may not be very strong. Even so, people in this context of government employment do tend to value the job stability, and when pushed to perform, they can be motivated to preserve their positions.

But even for private-sector jobs, the fact that some jobs provide better assurance of continued employment than others is a big motivator. In a small business, the risk may be very high that the company won't survive the next quarter of competition. In a big business, top management may decide to eliminate a division or a project, leaving the people involved out of work. So, for both small and large companies, when job security is higher, so also is job motivation.

Job stability in a company can be very motivating, when workers see that people in other companies are laid off more frequently. Well-paid jobs in natural resource extraction (e.g., oil drilling or coal mining) are often subject to temporary or permanent layoffs, which may make the paycheck less attractive than a smaller paycheck in a job that is more stable such as in a store or a bank or a telephone company. In a capitalist world where companies cannot count on government support to survive, there will always be some risk of the company failing or laying off people. But there are definitely some company jobs that are much more stable than others in all stages of a business cycle.

The Covid-19 pandemic of 2020–21 has demonstrated that many jobs are quite insecure, even if business had been stable or growing before the virus arrived. Once hospitality businesses such as restaurants and hotels had to shut temporarily, and then only open slowly after several months or longer, the employees saw how fragile their employment was. This led to widespread moves by these employees to other jobs even before the pandemic had diminished in severity. And it is likely that not all of those jobs will be reinstated once business returns to normal, since work has changed to allow more working from home, more meeting via videoconference, and thus less need for some of the hospitality services. This may be an overstatement, because even when working from home, people still go out to restaurants and consume many other services – although hotels may suffer for a considerably longer period of time as business travel remains below pre-pandemic levels.

Interesting, challenging work

The days of long hours working on an assembly line doing the same, narrow, boring activity all day long are long gone in most businesses. The person who placed the door on a car being assembled in Detroit has long ago been replaced by a robot. I am sure that somewhere this drudgery still exists, but today it is more a question of performing some tasks that do become very routine and do not offer much stimulation to the individual. Working in back-office recordkeeping may be today's equivalent of the assembly line, although even this recordkeeping is becoming more and more automated.

So, the challenge for the organization and the manager is to find opportunities for employees to vary their work, perhaps to work on different parts of the work process, and to keep them mentally involved. Maybe working as a hamburger-flipper at McDonalds – a classic example of low-skill, low-pay work today – is a better case to consider. The person who flips the hamburgers can easily be assigned to that task for some period of time, and then shifted to work on preparing other items such as coffee or milkshakes or some other food item. They can spend some time cleaning the restaurant, putting away items received from delivery trucks and performing lots of other small tasks. For some people, working at the cash register taking orders from people and delivering the orders when complete would be another task, although some employees surely would prefer to work in the meal preparation and not in the interpersonal part of the business dealing with customers. My point here is that even in very mundane jobs, there is opportunity for the manager to assign people to varied work, and to help them avoid the feeling of boredom or drudgery. This same idea applies to many other work environments, and to keep the employees motivated, the manager needs to figure out ways to keep the work interesting and challenging.

Opportunity for development

Even if the daily work environment is comfortable and enjoyable, people also need an ability to see if their work leads to opportunities for advancement. Not everyone wants to be the boss or the chief executive, but everyone does have interests in advancement of some sort, whether it be in salary, in job level, or even in opportunities to be involved in interesting and challenging projects or activities.

According to the second executive in a consumer products company, training, development and joining important meetings and decisions are a strong motivator. She said: "Currently I am organizing diversity, equity, and inclusion trainings in my new organization with 3 people from the Knowledge Center, and they are very eager and enthusiastic to learn, design and bring to a product to life".

And from another perspective, from a former banker and now small business owner:

> At both my career in banking and as a small business owner, my priority has been to try to find out what were my subordinates' requirements

to achieve their professional and life goals. Money and benefits were primary concerns for most of them, but usually there was at least one other component of their employment rewards that would be decisive in motivating them to help me achieve my own goals. These ranged from the opportunity to buy the business at a certain time, which has been the case in the last 5 years with the general manager of my auto repair business, to the case of a young secretary who was given the job title of assistant vice-president in exchange for not accepting a job offer with higher pay from another bank. Others want to work part-time with flexible hours to be able to attend university".

The priorities are different for the different workers, but the opportunity for personal development was a common theme.

Autonomy

People want the ability to do their jobs well without excessive supervision or observation. If the boss is constantly looking over your shoulder or telling you what to do or how to do it, the work environment is not attractive. People in all kinds of jobs and at all levels want to have some control of their activities, even as small as deciding what clothing to wear or what words to use in greeting a customer or client. It should be clear that no one person can do all of the work needed in an organization or a division, so different people have to deal with different tasks. And giving them room to pursue those tasks is the essence of autonomy.

It is very motivating to feel that you have the freedom to do a good job – or to make mistakes that you may learn from. Of course, there are situations when making mistakes can be disastrous to an organization, such as making major financial commitments. So significant oversight is needed in such situations. But with a few exceptions such as this, employees can generally be given the autonomy to carry out their work and to demonstrate their capabilities in doing so. Mistakes will happen, but learning results from those mistakes.

Fun

It may seem like a silly idea, but if a job offers a sense of fun, it is very likely to be more motivating than a job that is more mundane and perhaps boring. Fun can come in various guises, from silly activities such as foosball in the break room to playing pranks on each other to just sitting around a table discussing the business in a relaxed and non-challenging way. A Thursday afternoon session for an hour with your team to talk about how your business is doing and what wild new ideas could be tried out can be a tremendous amount of fun and potentially valuable thinking for the team. Remember the fact that most executives and managers at any level spend most of their time on routine issues. Breaking through with this kind of fun activity may really make a difference for coming up with new and innovative ideas.

Keeping people in a post-Covid world

How can you offer an attractive enough environment in your organization to keep people who otherwise might decide to move on during the "Great Resignation"? Since 2020 there has been a jump in people who have chosen alternative work styles, including changing jobs, as a result of many dramatic changes that have occurred during the pandemic. The fact that many people had to work from home, or at least remotely, during the pandemic has led many to choose to maintain that lifestyle even when businesses reopen and offices are operating again. Ian Cook (2021) found that resignations have been highest for people in the 30–45-year-old bracket, which means mid-career people, rather than the usual high turn-over for people in the 18–30-year-old group. It is more important than ever to offer an attractive work environment and to find motivators to keep your people.

While there is no guaranteed method to adjust a company's attractive-ness, other than to pursue the motivators discussed in this chapter and to aim for reducing the de-motivators discussed in the next chapter, still there are some ways to approach the problem in a focused way. First, the firm can look at turnover to identify which kinds of employees are leaving in greater numbers. Second, the characteristics of those employees such as job category, location, sex and age can be tabulated. Then the firm should consider the impact of the loss of these people on overall company performance. If they are the key people driving success of the company, then obviously imme-diate and carefully designed steps should be taken to try to retain them. Maybe it is compensation; maybe it is flexibility in location of work or in timing. If a particular category of employee who is leaving has less impact on overall organizational performance, then maybe less attention should be paid to them.

Given the fact that work is changing rapidly in the post-Covid era, the one sure thing is that organizations need to be quick to react to the changes and to be flexible in their work requirements. Even the defin-ition of 'post-Covid' is unclear. We may likely be in an era where Covid remains around the world as an illness, but where the deaths and dramatic social responses have dropped off greatly. The Great Resignation most likely will decrease as well, but it will be because companies figure out ways to motivate and retain their key employees with changes in the work environment.

Conclusions

There are many motivating factors that can get people to be more productive and more committed to their jobs. (Nohria et al. 2008 provide another set of motivation factors that can be pursued by the organization, similar to the factors discussed here.) One factor that often goes unrecognized is the simple tool of thanking people for their work, whether it is just the boss saying thank-you or a recognition ceremony or reward of some kind. These generally quite inexpensive gestures can really have far-reaching impacts on employees and on their satisfaction with the organization.

There are some factors that matter more in one culture than another, but which are still relevant everywhere. For example, the first consumer products company executive said,

> Encouraging junior employees to speak up and voice their ideas works especially well in Middle Eastern countries as most young people are taught not to speak when there are elders around. These younger people feel empowered and very motivated when they see and feel their opinions are valued and that they can make a meaningful contribution in the decision-making process.

People everywhere appreciate the opportunity to be heard, and in the times when their ideas are used by the organization, it is a superb motivating factor.

Perhaps a caveat is that money is not unimportant. People may say that income is not their main concern, and this may be true. But more than one issue is involved in creating a motivating environment, and compensation should not be ignored. People want to feel that their contributions are valuable, and that the company does value them explicitly. This is quite a complex issue, with concerns about fairness among people and comparability with other similar companies, bonuses versus salary increases and more elements. The point is that compensation is a necessary condition for motivating people, but, it in most cases, is not sufficient – requiring other factors as discussed in this chapter.

References

Bassett-Jones, Nigel, and Geffrey Lloyd, 2005. Does Herzberg's motivation theory have staying power? *Journal of Management Development*, 24(10), 929–43.

Cook, Ian, 2021. Who is driving the great resignation?. *Harvard Business Review* online. September 15.

Herzberg, Frederick, 2003. One more time: How do you motivate employees? *Harvard Business Review*. January. 2–13.

Nohria, Nitin, Boris Groysberg, and Linda-Eling Lee, 2008. Employee motivation: A powerful new model. *Harvard Business Review*, 86(7/8), 78–83.

Chapter 3

What de-motivates people?

Just as we looked at a variety of things that spur people on to greater productivity and commitment to the organization in the last chapter, we can look at things that de-motivate them as well. De-motivating practices include everything from criticism of a subordinate's work to failure to give people a sense of opportunity for future advancement or enjoyment of their work. Let's look at a number of these factors.

Criticism for mistakes or for doing a bad job

The opposite of praise for a job well done is criticism for a job poorly done. It actually may be that the downside of criticism is more damaging than the upside from praise is uplifting. When an employee fails to carry out a task well or otherwise demonstrates poor performance, the boss should not shy away from recognizing the lack of adequate performance. But the way in which a failure is recognized can be tremendously harmful to the person and organization if it does not lead to a desire for improvement. If recognition of failure is just carried out by criticizing the person's work or effort, then very possibly no constructive outcome may come about. If a criticism is accompanied by guidance on how to succeed the next time, or even hands-on coaching of the person to help them succeed, this style may very well be productive.

I experienced this phenomenon at the bank in South Africa, when I had to admonish a direct report for failing to meet a deadline on a clearly defined task. There was no good excuse for the failure, but at the same time I realized it was not useful to hammer the person for the recognized shortcoming. Instead, it was much more useful to talk with him about how to ensure that the next assignment would be completed successfully. This person was the meekest, nicest individual you could imagine, but he spent more time being nice to everyone and less in getting his job done than was healthy. We got along very well – he still asked me for recommendations years after we had gone to other jobs. I think that encouraging him to make a bigger effort to

DOI: 10.4324/9781003367512-3

meet deadlines and get work done was better than just criticizing him for failing to do those things – at least in our relations within the bank!

I should point out that I am a white North American and my direct report at the bank in this example was a black South African. I did not see any difference in this relationship when I had a white (South African) direct report who failed to meet a goal or a deadline. The individual people were different, but their response to criticism was very similar. Coating the criticism with a layer of coaching guidance for better results the next time was equally effective in both instances. You might anticipate that the white executive would have reacted more positively to the constructive criticism than his racially different colleague – but that was not my experience. People really are people!

I also had a quite striking experience at the university in Mexico, when two of my department heads had an argument, and they wanted my intervention to settle things. The one person had made a decision that incensed the other one. He admitted that he made a mistake, and apologized for it to her in front of me. But his colleague was still outraged, and seemed to want some kind of judgment against him. She would not let it go. I did the best that I could to soothe their feelings in our meeting, but I really did not have a solution. My 'brilliant' judgment was to admonish Raul for his decision that was hurtful to Maria, and then to send them both on their way.

Then, hours later, I saw the two of them in the lunchroom with arms over each other's shoulders, laughing and enjoying their mutual company and that of another half-dozen professors. I was really mystified as to how they could have overcome their seemingly extreme opposition to each other with this magical turnaround. I think that the answer is that I provided them a forum to hear each side of the story, and that was really all they wanted. I did not need to fire or penalize or even criticize anybody – it was just listening that mattered. This worked wonderfully, as both of them felt relieved that the confrontation was over, that I had intervened, and that life could go on as usual. How about that?

Let's turn the example around. You must have had an experience where you made a mistake or failed to get a job done, and your boss or teacher or parent criticized you for that failure. How did you feel? I am sure that if it was a simple criticism, without positive direction included, that you were devastated. You may be both ashamed that you did not perform as expected and also discouraged that the failure was called out by your trusted superior. Can't you see how a tiny adjustment to the criticism could improve your own reaction?

It really is devastating to have a weakness identified like that, especially without giving an opportunity to rectify the situation or to do better next time. The criticism may be 100% accurate, but the outcome can be much more positive if the person who failed is shown a direction to go that will fix the problem or help to avoid it in the future. This kind of solution is so much more useful than just identifying the problem. You will feel or you felt that the failure was true, but that your teacher or parent or boss was actually helpful if he/she offered guidance about what to do next time, rather than just pointing out the failure. You still may sting from the criticism, but the effects are not long-lasting if you immediately have a direction to go to do better next time.

It is just like when you tell your team that you don't want to hear about problems, but rather you want to hear about suggestions for how to resolve them. Don't tell me that your team is failing to meet work targets; tell me what could be done to achieve the goal. I really love that style of managing, even though it does not always work due to specific circumstances that may not allow for clear solutions. Anyway, you get the idea; it is better to give negative feedback and at the same time give the opportunity for dealing with the problem or just positive encouragement to deal with it the next time.

A senior banking executive found another way to help a subordinate who had a difficult time at his global bank. The subordinate was a soft-spoken, brilliant analytical type. This person never volunteered information at meetings and generally did not share his ideas or knowledge with others. The executive got him to succeed by grilling him outside of the context of meetings, so that he knew what the guy had to contribute, and was able to prompt him during meetings. This both added to the discussions in the meetings, and gave the person more confidence in his role and his contribution to the organization.

The consumer products executive noted that

> I managed Senior Vice Presidents and Vice Presidents plus General Managers in my career. It is very important to give fact-based reviews to all, but when they are senior, this becomes even more important. Non-U.S. cultures will show variety of reactions to negative feedback, but it is always important to give the feedback in a private setting, not in a group. That makes people upset. As long as it is in private, fact and example-based feedback will be understood. If you start with positives, then suggest improvements when discussing mistakes or weaknesses, it works well. Asking their own evaluation is also a good step where relevant.

The university executive with experience in the United States and in the United Arab Emirates said that:

> How criticism is communicated is vitally important, since a public dressing down or an unalloyed rebuke in private can be devastating and obviate any positive benefit that might have resulted from the criticism. I try even in the most serious cases to couch my criticisms within a shell of context, that is, to make sure that any positive elements of the

employee's behavior get full mention. This should not be construed as pulling one's punches. You want to leave the employee whole, however, and allow them to emerge from the session with their self-respect intact, their head held high.

Excellent advice!

Overwork/underpayment

One complaint that I have heard repeatedly over the years is that people are finding themselves with more work but not more pay. A common example is when one of your colleagues leaves the company for another job, or by retiring, or by moving to a different division – and then that person is not replaced. So you, or I, are left with picking up the work that was previously done by our departed colleague, without adding a replacement person. What can you do? Obviously, you should try to get your superior(s) to hire a replacement person, and not simply to divide the work among existing people who already have full-time responsibilities. Even if the organization has the intent to replace a lost employee, it still will take some time to do so, and the burden has to be placed on somebody at least temporarily. This is a burden that usually can be dealt with in good faith for a (short) period of time while a replacement is found. However, increasingly I see that companies try to reduce headcount without reducing the workload on those who remain. This is not a sustainable strategy.

It is certainly true that machines and software can replace some manpower/womanpower in the workplace. And this does happen repeatedly as technology advances. So, this can reduce the added burden on people when a colleague leaves the organization or the division. But at the end of the day you may still be left with greater responsibilities and no change in work conditions or compensation. So, the de-motivation factor is real, and it is something that both employee and company should aim to eliminate – through appropriate staffing and through efforts by the employee to make the burden known.

Even without a change in personnel as in the above example, you may find that your workload increases due to growing numbers of clients or new responsibilities that arise with technology change or new regulation or some other unanticipated need. Now what? This kind of situation is extremely common, and the organization needs to find some way to reduce the feeling of overburdening people in this instance as well. While it is in principle possible to adjust the staffing of an organization to deal with growing demand for its products or services, the adjustment is not automatic and more often than not the situation leaves some employees overburdened and dissatisfied.

What you can do as a boss is to try to see the changing conditions and observe the pressures being placed on people. When you see that work is piling up on someone due to the growing business or loss of other employees, the de-motivation is clear, and you need to do something about it. That something is probably to hire another person, or perhaps to find some automation that can reduce the burden on the person in question. In addition, it is crucial to demonstrate to that person that you understand the unfair burden and that you are doing something about it. I found that in the bank, I almost always had to try to get permission to add to head count – or steal someone away from another division who was underutilized. At the university I found that compensation was based on the number of courses being taught. So, if someone needed to teach additional students, they could be assigned an additional course – and additional pay – and this usually solved the immediate problem. If the number of customers (students) continued on a higher level, then additional teachers were needed and this was seen to be fair.

Underpayment by itself is a more complicated problem. If an employee feels that she is underpaid because someone in the organization is doing a similar job for higher pay, perhaps some direct remedy is needed. More often than not I found that an individual would perceive his work to be more valuable than his pay for either subjective reasons or because people in other organizations were being paid more. This can be a very tricky problem. In the service-sector organizations that I know best, other similar institutions tend to have similar pay structures, and one person is seldom far out of line. When an obvious pay gap does exist, the organization should eliminate it. When the gap is in the mind of the employee, the organization cannot really be held responsible, and it is up to the boss to assuage the person in some way other than salary. This can be through praise or encouragement or even perks such as an opportunity to pursue a training program or participate in a conference somewhere interesting.

Lack of purpose or disorganization

Another aspect of the job environment that de-motivates employees is a sense of lack of purpose or lack of importance of what they are doing. You can easily imagine this problem if you work in some service business such as a hotel or restaurant or even a retail store. What value are you really adding to anyone's life or to society more broadly? This is quite an existential challenge, although one that can be handled by a creative boss who looks for ways to identify value in what an employee is doing. That value can be in making customers happy, or in creating a masterful service, such as a beautiful landscape if you work in mowing lawns or gardening, or a spotless kitchen if you work in a restaurant, or just creating an environment where customers enjoy coming to your business because of the friendly way they are treated.

It is very easy for an organization to slot people into jobs or tasks that need to be done, but which are not clearly identified for their purpose or importance. The boss should identify what employees value, and make sure that tasks are aligned with those values as much as possible (Clark and Saxberg 2019). This may be as easy as having conversations with employees to see what their interests are and what their self-conceptions are, so that tasks can be described in relation to those factors.

A senior executive at a financial services company, says that he has found that people are greatly de-motivated by a lack of clarity of what is expected of them. People hate to be surprised at their year-end review when something unexpected comes up related to their performance. He has found this response to be consistent across people in the United States, Latin America, the United Kingdom and Europe, where he has had assignments over the years. The boss needs to respond to this challenge and clarify the work.

Ignoring achievements and also ignoring poor performance

A striking example of behavior that will de-motivate people in an organization that has nothing to do with money is the failure to recognize achievements – and at the same time failure to recognize poor performance. We talked earlier about how praise and recognition are positive influences on people. Failing to provide that feedback is likely to lead the deserving person to feel underappreciated and unfulfilled. So, the use of praise/recognition is not only a motivator, but its absence is potentially a severe detriment to the organization. It is pretty obvious how to deal with this de-motivating factor – use praise and recognition!

If criticism for poor performance is necessary but possibly a deterrent to motivation, then simply avoiding criticism sounds like a solution. But it is a terrible solution, because those who escape a reckoning for their poor performance will not be encouraged to do any better. And what's worse, this kind of treatment will discourage others when they see that culprits avoid punishment or criticism. The solution is to find ways to convey the criticism in a manner that provides the recipient a positive way to respond. And this is almost always done in a private way, such that other people are not present or involved. The criticism needs to be delivered one-on-one, and the guidance for better performance likewise, preferably in one discussion.

This is probably true in many kinds of organization, but especially in the professional services ones such as management consulting, advertising, accounting, university-level teaching, medical service provision, financial services provision and information technology. The experts (professionals) in these fields typically each think that they are smarter than everyone else. Or at least that they are very smart. So, in conveying criticism to such a person, you really have to focus on getting the point across and then offering substantial guidance and support for improving the behavior/performance. You don't want to leave such a person feeling beaten down, because the reaction may well be to reject the criticism and look for ways to escape the situation/organization rather than to improve performance.

This issue may seem paradoxical: if people want to feel that the organization treats them fairly, presumably that means they want to be treated the same as other people. That is correct as far as equality of treatment with respect to opportunities, human resources benefits and general fairness are concerned. However, if a leader tries to treat all of her subordinates the same despite their differences in performance, then that would be a mistake. And being treated the same as my co-worker when I have done a much better job is a tremendously de-motivating behavior by the boss.

Uncertainty

Doubts about the future can have a debilitating effect on people. When Covid-19 hit in 2020, people everywhere did not know how severe the pandemic would be nor how long it would last. The most recent similar experience occurred in 1918 with the Spanish flu that killed over 50 million people worldwide and about 675,000 in the United States alone. Since that was about 100 years ago, it was very difficult to draw any conclusions about your risk in the Covid-19 pandemic. We know at this point that under 7 million people have died from the virus worldwide, so that it appears to have about 1/10 the impact of the Spanish flu. However, within the United States there have already been over one million deaths from Covid-19, which is not very different from the pandemic a century ago. Whether this is good or bad is not the point. The uncertainty of whether or not you would get the virus and how severe it would be if you became infected is the challenge.

So, how can an organization deal with this kind of uncertainty – which to this day remains a question? To make employees feel more comfortable, initially it was judged that working from home, when possible, was a good strategy for avoiding the virus. This of course ignores the millions of jobs, particularly in service sectors, that require physical presence to provide the service. The choices available to companies were very different, depending on the business. Then, if it was possible to have people work from home, this model turned out to be a strain on organizations for many reasons. It is difficult to maintain an enthusiasm among people if they never see each other (in real terms, not on a screen). Work from home tends to be more overwhelming because it is easy to spend more time on work than if work/home life is separated. And work from home creates conflicts between personal activities and work, especially when living at home with a family or just with other people in general. The solution to this set of challenges is not yet known, although many companies and other organizations are trying various alternatives, even as more people get vaccinated and the virus is having less impact on people's activities.

What about the uncertainty of whether a new technology might displace your key product, or if a new market entrant might take your company's customers or if weather conditions will make your business suffer from lack of rain or extreme heat or a hurricane? Of course, you can buy insurance and look for ways to diversify, but the point here is about how the people within the organization are affected. If an employee can escape a situation with high uncertainty by leaving the job, it is very likely that the company runs a risk of losing that person.

In fact, no one likes uncertainty of these types. It is one thing to say that some countries and cultures are more willing to accept higher levels of uncertainty (e.g., according to Hofstede's measure, people from Greece, Portugal and Latin American countries are highly averse to uncertainty, whereas people from Singapore, Jamaica and Scandinavian countries are very willing to live with uncertainty. The United States is close to the low-risk-averse end of the scale.) But no one is enthusiastic about having a high risk of being laid off, whether due to business conditions, the pandemic or other factors.

Another senior executive in a consumer products company noted:

> In my experience, uncertainty and ambiguity are the top two demotivators for employees – regardless of their backgrounds, race, religion, and geography they are from. This is especially true in larger corporate settings vs startups where uncertainty and ambiguity are expected and welcomed. ... The best way to tackle these issues is open, honest, and timely communication. It may not always be possible to share all details or confidential information. However, it always works when people believe they are kept in the loop, and when they get clear and concise information. It is critical to be as concise, honest and straightforward as possible in performance reviews with tangible examples for each positive and negative assessment. Nuance is in the way to deliver the same information across different cultures – tone of voice, time spent for Q&A, etc.

Some valuable thoughts for us all.

Lack of opportunity for development

While it is usually not a daily grind on people, still from time to time they think about advancement in their careers or just in their job activities. If you are an assistant in your job, it is natural to want to eventually become the manager or the lead person in that particular activity. If you are a junior manager, it is logical that you should want to become a senior manager, or an executive, or whatever other title might apply to a person as she moves up in the organization. Even for professional services an accountant starts off with some title implying a junior level, and works up to a senior title such as Partner in a firm organized as a partnership.

When it is not clear in the organization how a person can move up in rank or responsibility or even just in the perception of others, then a problem exists. Some people thrive on aiming for such goals – and they will be greatly de-motivated when the possibility to move up is either not there or is not clear. Even people who do not have a strong wish to move up in the organization still need a structure that lets them know where they stand and how the organization hierarchy works. Failing to provide the opportunity and the guidelines is a very real problem.

In all of the organizations where I have worked – in banking, academia, government, postal service, retail stores and consulting – the job hierarchy was clear and the paths to advancement were at least identified if not easily achieved. By this I mean that in many or most jobs, as you move up in the organization, there are fewer people at the higher level. So, some people must be moved out of the organization over time, as they lose the competition with others to move up. This does not have to be a dog-eat-dog kind of competition, but as you move up the ranks thin out. This is true even in organizations like the military, where some people may wish to spend their entire career, but where advancement opportunities have to be limited as anywhere else. This means that the problem of designing a plan for advancement is key to almost any organization, and the leaders should think through the plan and its implications for morale of the workforce very carefully.

Combining this point with a couple of other de-motivators, the senior executive from the consumer products firm said:

> One of the key demotivators is not having a clear vision, goals and changing evaluation criteria continuously. The other is not being able to contribute as an individual. People's main objective to join an organization is to contribute and in return get paid and develop. If they do not have clear goals and opportunity to contribute, then they get demotivated and not engaged. Soon they depart. Being valuable as an individual in a purposeful organization is key in most cultures. Having your voice heard whatever your style is, having an inclusive environment and getting the message regularly that we care about you are critical motivators.

My boss is a jerk – poor management style

I remember very clearly that my job at the bank in leadership development was launched after a workplace survey had shown that quite a few people felt that their bosses were not the kind of leaders that they wanted. Or in other words, 'my boss is a jerk'. The bank decided to devote time and resources to respond to this de-motivating situation. The program that was put in place ended up taking three years and putting more than 10,000 managers and executives through a two-week leadership course with outside instructors and a range of added bells and whistles.[1] This is not recommended for every organization, but it was a carefully designed effort to deal with the de-motivation.

This effort at the bank definitely did not change the organization completely, or turn all bosses into great leaders. But I think that some bosses did indeed improve their management of subordinates through the experience, and many, many people felt encouraged that the bank cared enough about them to offer this opportunity. A huge lesson may be that just demonstrating that an organization does care about its people is a very valuable, positive motivating force.

Perhaps even more than caring for the people, the organization simply paid attention to them. There are many ways to accomplish this goal, from rewards to opportunities like this training course to simple individual meetings between a boss and a direct report, without any evaluation purpose. That is, just a meeting maybe once a month with each subordinate on the team or in the organization may serve to indicate the company's interest in everybody.

The university executive made this comment about avoiding the bad-boss syndrome:

> Whatever deprives employees of their sense of ownership of their work, of their pride in their product tends, in my experience, to de-motivate. For the manager as perfectionist, this requirement of good management can be tremendously difficult. Managers who cannot accept that colleagues may deliver a product, a report, an analysis that is at variance with what the manager had in mind risk becoming micromanagers, and micro-management is worse than underpay or red tape as a demotivator. Overcoming the need to place my fingerprints on everything my direct-reports did was the hardest lesson I had to learn when I moved into senior management. Having a boss who corrects your every sentence or rearranges every chart in a presentation is deadly. Next time, you are less likely to give the job your best efforts so as to avoid the embarrassment of having your work micro-critiqued to the point where it is no longer recognizable as your own. Not helpful.

This is excellent guidance for bosses – though it may be difficult to carry out for many people.

Red tape and unnecessary rules; lack of empowerment

We like to complain about government regulations and the red tape that they impose on everyone for getting a tax refund, or a driver's license renewal or this past couple of years for getting a Covid-19 payment for lost work or lost business. This kind of bureaucracy also exists in companies, as much as we might like to deny it.

Think about taking a trip or having a meal with a client to carry out the company's business. How long does it take to get reimbursed, and how much documentation do you need to present? How about getting help with interpretation and payment of your health benefits? In medium-sized and large companies, as well as other organizations, these processes can be tremendously time-consuming and tedious. And in this era of electronic payments, you have to look at your bank account much later to see if the reimbursement payment had been made. This is really a pain!

It may be a separate debate about whether or not these processes are necessary, but surely in many cases they are. So, you just have to live with the red tape. Even if you get a job elsewhere, you are not likely to escape these kinds of rules. Some employers definitely make it easier than others. Non-government employers by and large have much less red tape in the processes noted above in comparison with government offices or agencies. But there is no escaping some amount of recordkeeping and report filing.

What can a company do to reduce the de-motivating aspects of this problem? Certainly, the easiest thing is to keep red tape to a minimum. This is easy to say, but in some instances it is difficult to reduce or eliminate the paperwork that is required for reporting to tax authorities and other government agencies. Even so, there are many procedures that develop over time in an organization, and from time to time it is important to take a careful look at them and to eliminate rules and steps that are no longer needed or are just too complicated to justify.

Poor communication

Just as we talk about how implementation is a crucial part of designing a company's strategy, it is equally important to communicate that strategy, both within the company and to the external world. The same idea applies to employee motivation. Unless you tell people what the company is doing and where it is headed, they will tend to get caught up in their day-to-day work and lose sight of the bigger picture. This is hugely important in building that *esprit de corps* that you want in an organization, and it is not that difficult to accomplish. It is a question of communication – and if you fail to communicate successfully, employee morale and commitment is sure to suffer (e.g., Spitzer 1995).

This problem is particularly challenging in a professional services organization, where the experts tend to work intensively on their own projects with their own or assigned clients. People in this context do not have time to sit back and think about where the organization is going or what challenges may be affecting it. Leaders need to communicate the direction of the company, the way that people's work fits into that direction and also to alert people about challenges such as regulatory hurdles, shareholder or stakeholder concerns, or even simple things like moving to different offices. It is extremely discouraging to a professional person when the company's travel policy is changed or some recordkeeping rule changes without informing the person ahead of time and giving at least in principle a chance to voice objection or opinions.

Summing up

There are many kinds of action or condition or style that affect a person's experience at work, and the employer needs to think through them all and try to ensure that the environment is attractive to the employees. It is probably impossible to anticipate all of the de-motivating factors that could occur to sidetrack employees, but hopefully this chapter has identified many of the key ones, and has offered some ideas about how to deal with them. Those things that de-motivate people in some instances are the opposite of things that motivate people, such as criticism versus praise. But many of the de-motivating factors are different, such as uncertainty. You cannot have certainty for many things in life or in business. But creating an environment that is predictable can assuage some of the unpredictability, and this can eliminate a de-motivating factor. So, creating the predictable environment can reduce the negative, while by itself this environment is not likely to be enough to motivate employees. The issues raised in this chapter are de-motivators, which can be dealt with in the various specific ways that are presented, and as reinforced by the experiences of senior executives.

Note

1 One element was that each person who experienced the training course was required to spend one day during that year in a community service project such as building a Habitat for Humanity house or working in an AIDS orphanage or a school. This was very well received by the participants, once they got into it.

References

Clark, Richard, and Bror Saxberg, 2019. 4 Reasons good employees lose their motivation. *Harvard Business Review Online.* https://hbr.org/2019/03/4-reasons-good-employees-lose-their-motivation

Spitzer, Dean, 1995. The seven deadly demotivators. *Management Review*, 84(11) (November), 56–60.

Chapter 4

Trust

How do you create trust between people?

While this idea may seem fairly simple, there really is no single way to ensure that one person will trust another. If William Tell places an apple on your head and promises to shoot it off with a bow and arrow from 120 paces, you would really have to be extremely trusting to go along with that![1] But in a more mundane context, how can you get people in your organization to trust you? This may come just from day-to-day dealings in which you are truthful in talking with them. You probably can just tell them about things like future deadline dates for delivering or receiving reports, or about some other factual points that will show over time that you are truthful. You can also share things like the company's profit outlook or growth plans, and they most likely would trust that you are telling the truth – even though you cannot know the future and whether the plans really will play out. As long as you do not have a history of telling lies and being caught doing so, you probably have a very good chance that people will trust your statements on these kinds of things.

The issue of trust, and its impact on workers' commitment to a company, has been studied fairly extensively. One well-known example is that of David Packard (1995), who said that when he worked at General Electric, the company had kept its tools and parts under close watch, to make sure that employees did not steal anything. He found this so degrading that when he and Bill Hewlett started HP, they set a policy of always leaving parts and storage areas open, to demonstrate trust in the employees. At least anecdotally, this generated a very positive team spirit at HP, which has lasted through the decades.

The executive in management consulting said that they establish trust by having extremely clear principles on how decisions (about salaries, bonuses and assignments) are made. And then the company consistently delivers as promised. This set of clear rules and transparency in following them creates a trusting culture in the firm. Parallel to this system is the effort to establish

DOI: 10.4324/9781003367512-4

trust between a supervisor and his/her direct reports. That interpersonal trust is key at the firm, and it has been maintained as a foundation of its successful operation over the years. Knowing that your supervisor 'has your back' is an extremely reassuring element of working in an intensely competitive environment.

A relatively new challenge at this firm is to evaluate performance of specialists in areas such as information technology and law. Historically, almost all of the consultants were generalists, and terms of reference for evaluation were made long ago and then passed down over time. When specialists have joined the firm, new bases for evaluation have been needed. So, the original process of establishing terms of reference for each type of specialist have been set – but the process of getting to those criteria was a source of some lack of trust for the newcomers, who are not evaluated on the same terms as the generalists.

What about trust on more sensitive subjects? When we entered the global financial crisis in late 2008, I had to tell people in my division at the bank in South Africa that they would not be laid off. This was a conscious decision of the CEO and the executive committee to ensure that no one would be fired due to the business downturn for at least one year. Each of us division heads had to share the news with our teams. Of course, the goal was to reassure people that the sky was not falling, even though our business was declining significantly. The idea in making the decision was that (1) we expected the crisis to end within a year, and (2) if it continued beyond that, then we might have to lay off some people. Also, natural attrition from retirements and voluntary job changes, without replacing most of those people, cut our employment by about 1–2% during the year anyway. The bank survived, and at least I think that people tended to trust what we said about keeping everyone employed.

You could fast forward this experience to the Covid-19 pandemic. Many organizations had to tell employees that they would not be able to continue working since the restaurant or hotel or transport company was not allowed to operate for an uncertain period of time due to public health concerns. The companies could promise to rehire people, or take them off of forced 'vacations' when conditions would improve – but there was certainly no idea when that would be. Being honest might generate trust – but it did not solve the uncertainty! The pandemic has been a very difficult challenge, but fortunately it is one that has only occurred once previously in the past century and is not likely to recur frequently in the future.

I was working in a university at that time, and the statement from the President in May was that we would not lay off people during 2020 after the virus had hit back in March. From my observation at least, this statement was widely believed and was greatly reassuring to employees. When our student enrollment numbers actually increased in the Fall semester of 2020,[2] the university's commitment to the employees was possible to continue, since revenues did not decline. Although costs did go up when instruction had to be moved completely online (mostly through Zoom), and both equipment costs and training were needed to operate successfully online. Even so, the reassurance was highly successful, and it appeared to me that people did trust the President's statements about avoiding job reductions.

Consider the situation for the hotel/hospitality industry when Covid struck. For Hilton, which offers nearly a million rooms in more than 6,200 properties across 118 countries, second-quarter revenue per available room, a key financial metric in the hotel industry, tumbled 81% from the same period a year ago, as the company swung to a net loss of $430 million from net income of $260 million. As travel restrictions and lockdown measures spread across the globe, Hilton was forced to play defense, by temporarily closing hotels, furloughing employees, cutting salaries and other costs, and borrowing money to provide some financial breathing room. "Never in Hilton's 101-year history has our industry faced a global crisis that brings travel to a virtual standstill", Chief Executive Christopher Nassetta said in June (Marketwatch 2020).

How could the hotel operator create trust among employees under these conditions? Well, not very easily. One 'good' feature of the situation was that the major hotel chains such as Marriott and Hilton mostly franchise out their hotel facilities – so the parent company did not have to lay off all of the hotel workers. Even so, Hilton and Marriott do own some of their branded hotels, and they did have to deal with the fallout from the pandemic lockdowns and quarantine issues. Marriott said in May 2020:

> furloughs and reduced work week schedules which began in April will be extended through October 2, 2020. Marriott is also rolling out a voluntary transition program for on-property and above-property associates in the United States who may choose to leave the company to pursue other opportunities. Similar voluntary programs are being considered in other parts of the world. Given the company's expectation that prior levels of business will not return until beyond 2021, the company anticipates a significant number of above-property position eliminations later this year. The company is not able at this time to predict how many associates will be affected by these separations or any resulting charges or cost savings.
> (https://news.marriott.com/news/2020/05/27/statement-on-marriott-internationals-covid-19-update-to-associates)

This is not a very trust-generating statement for employees – but at the same time it was realistic and it gave a clear signal to employees that major cutbacks were taking place and would continue. I find this statement to be clear and responsive to the pandemic, even though hotel workers could not find much positive to say about "voluntary transition programs".

A facilities management company executive in South Africa said that:

> All our hospitality contracts were suspended during Covid. We needed
> to make some choices with the people, bearing in mind that we wanted
> to minimize job losses/retrenchments but also ensure business con-
> tinuity and sustainability. Our first thoughts were, and we managed, to
> successfully redeploy a large number of cleaners onto other contracts
> and into one-off Covid touch point cleaning services. We did a quick
> 1-week training program for touch-point cleaning, the use of PPE, the
> mitigation of being infected, etc. and redeployed almost 80% of our
> workforce into other industries, such as mining and retail cleaning (e.g.
> supermarkets). Where we could not redeploy people, we registered them
> for Temporary Employee/Employer Relief Scheme (TERS) benefits
> which made up the shortfall in their earnings to some degree, where
> there was a need. In addition we introduced and funded a scheme to
> the value of ZAR 2,000 [about $US 150] per month for lower level
> workers and also paid for statutory benefits. We also did give the affected
> employees an option to earn a part of their salaries or take retrenchment
> packages. The take up was: 30% took the retrenchment packages and
> the remaining 70% elected to work even at a reduced overall salary. It
> goes to show – changing jobs at these levels is quite difficult, which has
> exacerbated the unemployment rate for semi-skilled employees. It will
> take some years to get this back to normal, and will be heavily reliant
> on economic growth.
>
> Our hospitality operations (catering and lounges) however, took a
> huge knock as we had to retrench almost 70% of our workforce as all
> operations were closed. They did qualify for Unemployment Benefits.
> Once we started to reopen we contacted the retrenched employees
> first to give them the option for reemployment. About 70% did re-join.
>
> It was a very difficult and trying time for all of us, trying to balance
> the sustainability of the businesses with the needs of the people. We
> tried to minimize job losses, which I think we did quite well with,
> and also took advantage of government and Group assistance, which
> was a tremendous help. I must also add that we did have almost 200
> deaths in these businesses directly related to Covid infections. Some
> of these positions were critical and we are still recovering from the
> loss of these skills and intellectual property. Lots of lessons learned,
> and I guess we will be better prepared for these types of events into
> the future.

Hopefully, the kind of health crisis will not occur again for another century,
just like the last time.

Demonstrate your own trust

Separate from these cataclysmic situations, how do you build trust between people in an organization? Over a period of years you can demonstrate credible behavior, such that people will come to trust your word and your deeds. As noted by the oil and gas executive, "the 'Deeds not Words' saying is certainly a cornerstone to building trust". To establish trust in the first place requires some demonstration of trustworthiness. This could be as simple as promising a raise or a bonus to your team members if a particular goal is met – and then following through as promised. The raise would only happen on the annual cycle, most likely, so a bonus that is paid right away would be more convincing. Or promising to give someone a nicer office or a project assignment that they are very interested in. The item being promised may be small or financially easily manageable, but the meaning of the promise and upholding it can be a source of long-lasting trust.

You could offer a person the opportunity to work without overbearing supervision, demonstrating your trust in them. This should be the case in general, but sometimes it turns out that offering a person a task to accomplish and then just letting them go for it can be a liberating experience. During the Covid-19 pandemic this kind of letting go was common, as people had to work from home and bosses could not supervise with nearly as much diligence. Of course, there have been many examples of micromanagement from a distance, as bosses get a sense of losing control because people are not physically together in the office (e.g., Parker et al. 2020). Regardless, this idea of allowing people more space to carry out their assigned tasks has very often produced quite positive results in both performance and trust during the pandemic. Parker et al. (2020) suggest that one way to escape this problem of micromanagement is to train managers to manage by results, rather than by trying to manage by overseeing workers' activities on a frequent or constant basis.

According to the oil and gas executive, who recently opened a start-up company,

> I believe transparency is the biggest source of trust. Visibility to the big picture is the number one factor to creating trust. Sharing visibility to financials and results as they are in-process, key decision-making criteria and projects, and why the team is doing the things they are doing is what I've found creates trust. My startup has been actively looking to raise corporate equity for the past 9 months, and we have not taken on any outside capital because the terms provided by financial sponsors to date have not been in our acceptable strike zone (they either want too much control over our team, or ask for more equity than we are willing to give up). My employees know our cash reserves are shrinking because I show them the bank account balance each month, but I also tell them

why we are better off without the wrong financial partner, and they appreciate the visibility. It creates a "we're all in the same boat" feeling, which not only fosters trust, but also pushes people to take action to add value because they see where they can help out. This has taken the form of employees taking the initiative to seek ways for us to either sell incremental services or project/product work, or partner with a strategic partner who will pre-pay us for more of the work we are currently providing them, and at a more strategic level that will allow us to avoid selling any piece of our business.

Another way to demonstrate your trust is simply by helping people in some way. If you can offer guidance to a team member, without appearing overbearing, this can be a good basis for trust building. If you can pick up someone's kids on the way home from school when the colleague has some conflict that comes up, this certainly will demonstrate your willingness to help, and your trustworthiness. If you can help a new person get settled into the office or store and so forth, that will demonstrate concern for them, and it may be the beginning of a trusting relationship. There are many ways to take steps to establish trust, almost all of which are simple steps that can go a long way.

Be honest; admit mistakes

It seems almost silly to say it, but if you are honest with people, and they perceive that this is true, then you will be on the way to creating trust. It seems silly because you presumably would want to be honest anyway. I am sure that there are liars and dishonest people out there, but the vast majority of us are not. So, the challenge is to find ways to demonstrate honesty. I have found that it primarily comes from statements that you make about general business in the organization. If you don't hide things, and you tell the same story to everyone, then you will appear honest. This is easily seen in giving people feedback about their work. If you tell everyone that they are doing a great job, this is not possible, and making such statements will lead people to disbelieve you – unless you give everyone stellar performance evaluations every year! You don't have to offer devastating criticism of anyone, but differentiated performance evaluations according to actual performance outcomes are needed.

You probably won't have many situations where you may be caught out lying about something, so the issue of honesty will be more subtle, as in the happy-face comments that everyone is doing a great job. Think of another aspect of business that often leads to a leader making a questionable statement. It is a common trap for managers to present a view of things in the company that is too optimistic, in the attempt to make people feel comfortable. If a manager says that everything is rosy, and then the next month lays off three or four people, this is a contradictory signal. If the manager says that business is good, when the next week the company announces that sales have fallen, this is contradictory. The point is not that the manager necessarily lied about the situation, but that he/she should not have made a statement in the first place if there was no basis for the optimism. Being realistic is better than being unjustifiably positive.

You also need to be able to admit mistakes in your work or in your judgment. I have had many occasions when my judgment about a situation with a client or a supplier or a person in the organization has been wrong. It is difficult to admit such failings, because you tend to have the feeling that you are weak or inadequate because of such things. But that is just the time when you need to explicitly recognize the mistake, perhaps the reason that you made the mistake, apologize for it, and then move on. Nobody is perfect and no one expects perfection. Leaders too often feel the need to hide mistakes or blame them on someone else, when simply admitting the mistake will demonstrate honesty and can help generate trust in the person and in the organization.

Be transparent in decision-making

When you decide to go after a new market segment for your service, the best way to get employee buy-in is to involve them in this decision. Put the idea up for discussion in a team meeting, and listen to perspectives from around the room. If you cannot get a reasonable level of support for the idea, then maybe it is better not to proceed. Or better yet, you might talk with one or two key thought leaders on the team beforehand about the idea, to see if you can get them to join your side of the decision. If you enter the subsequent meeting with some support lined up, you are much more likely to get a positive outcome from the team. Your decision-making is much better informed by getting this input from other people, even if you ultimately feel the need to go against some other people's points of view.

This is especially true in a professional services organization, when you have a group of experts (lawyers, accountants, consultants, IT specialists) who need to support a chosen direction for the firm. It is like the famous chore of herding cats – getting highly independent people to agree on anything is a major task. So it makes a lot of sense to pre-seed the discussion with the views of a small number of people who are consulted beforehand. If you can get them to agree with your intended direction, it will be much easier to form a consensus around that direction, even if some people in the team will not agree with it.

In any organization transparency is a valuable tool. If you just explain the logic for your decisions, you will find much greater buy-in from the employees. If you lay out the facts that underlie a decision, that will generally bring people along to support the direction you want to go. You also may discover, in laying out the facts, that you missed something important that another person brings up. You may have missed a competitor's product or service that affects your own. You may have missed a regulatory barrier that needs to be dealt with. You even may have missed some existing commitment within your own company that makes your intended decision more complicated. This input can help you avoid mistakes that otherwise would have occurred.

Give them opportunity to work without supervision – demonstrate trust

A great way to gain the trust of others is to demonstrate your trust in them. A very simple way to do this is to assign some fairly well-defined task to a person, and ask that it be completed by a stated time, such as the end of the day. If you then allow the person to carry out that task, without supervision, it may easily give that person the sense that you trust them, and that you believe in their ability to do the job. The task may be something like updating a client list with new information, or communicating with external vendors to make sure that deliveries are going to be received on time. It should not be too trivial, nor something that requires a lot of interaction with the boss to verify that the work is being done correctly. If that balance is achieved in defining the task, a trusting relationship will be underway when the person delivers the results.

People tend to prefer to have some degree of control over their own work activities (as well as over their lives outside of work!). This may not be much of an issue for a McDonald's hamburger flipper or a hotel room cleaner, where the work is very routine. But even for them, when a person finds a way to do something more efficiently or better in some way, they should be heard by the organization and offered the opportunity to implement their ideas if they are useful. It is human nature for people to think that they have a better or simpler way to do things – but it is often the case that unrecognized factors don't in fact allow that other way to actually work out. It is up to the boss to distinguish between many good ideas that are not helpful from those few ideas that very well may save the company money or make the employee's job easier or more fun.

Meals and entertainment together; spending time together

What else can be done to stimulate a feeling of trust in the organization? Separate from trusting the boss and the organization, it is important to try to foster trust among the members of that organization. Activities such as team-building exercises may help. Just encouraging people to have lunch together or to come together once a week during the workday to share ideas, thoughts, experiences and so forth, can be very helpful in building trust. The more people get to know each other, the more likely it is for them to develop trusting relationships.

This is the same logic that says: as people from two different countries get to know each other better, through international trade or through any kind of cross-national association, the less likely they are to have disputes or even war between them. It is one of the foundations of the European Union, started after World War II when leaders wanted to find ways to get Germany and France to build peaceful relations and avoid another war. Creating trade links and organizations that connected people from the two countries made them more aware of their common interests and with trade expansion, they saw a common benefit from free trade that created more jobs in both countries. As William Schurz, President of the Thunderbird School of Global Management, said after World War II, "borders frequented by trade seldom need soldiers".

A senior executive at one of the top four US banks, and CEO of another financial services company after that, worked in several European locations. When he was 25 years old he was assigned to lead Diners Club Germany for the bank. He did not speak German, and he felt that a crucial element of success was to be able to communicate well with his team and to generate empathy with them from his interactions. He took intensive German lessons and almost from the start conducted his meetings in German. By demonstrating his willingness to make mistakes in the language – but also to learn it well – he won over the local people, and they trusted him to do a good job. This example illustrates not only the idea of building team cohesion through working together, but also the boss's willingness to admit mistakes and to focus on the issue of communication.

Spending time together does not mean forcing teams of people to have a Friday afternoon trip to the local bar or pub each week to relax after work, or to require people to have lunch together in the company cafeteria. Those kinds of forced interaction are likely to alienate people because of the extra burden on them, rather than building camaraderie. Just making the day more enjoyable by providing, say, a half-hour break in the midafternoon on Wednesdays can lead people to congregate together by choice, without forcing anything other than to return to work after the half hour. I don't want to say that this is the magic potion for getting people to build more trust or to enjoy their workday more, but it should move exactly in that direction. And you likely have additional ideas about what works or could work in your organization.

Make people feel like contributors; give them the opportunity to learn

Paul Zak (2017) noted that "high engagement – defined largely as having a strong connection with one's work and colleagues, feeling like a real contributor, and enjoying ample chances to learn – consistently leads to positive outcomes for both individuals and organizations" (p.4). He cites the Gallup Employee Engagement Survey, deployed over more than ten years and including literally millions of people, showing these outcomes.[3] He argues that building a culture of trust by providing these features is the source of the positive results.

This idea of making people feel like real contributors indicates the importance of feeling that what you do makes a difference. I was going to say that this is even more important today than 20 or 30 years ago, now that Millennials are becoming leaders in organizations, and we see their greater commitment to environmental protection, fairness among people, and other social goals in comparison with older generations. However, in checking studies on employee motivations, I discovered that there is very little difference in what people look for in a job today versus what they said they wanted years ago. In one study at Facebook (Goler et al. 2018), the authors found essentially no difference in attributes sought by people in their 20s, 30s, 40 or 50s. They all wanted career first (viz., a job that provides autonomy, allows you to use your strengths and encourages learning), community second (viz., feeling respected, cared about and recognized) and cause third (viz., feeling like you do some good in the world). This survey was done at just one employer, with about 50,000 employees, but it is consistent with other evidence about people's interest in a job.

This finding is consistent with evidence on job switching activity by people of different ages over time. The US Department of Labor carries out an annual survey of employee tenure with the current employer, and in this survey people in various age categories from 16 to 65 have demonstrated essentially the same length of stay with the employer since the survey that was done in 1983. That is, for example, people 25–34 years old stayed with their employer for 3.0 years on average in 1983, and they stayed for an average of 2.8 years in 2020. For people aged 55–64, they stayed with their employer for 12.2 years in 1983 and for 10.3 years in 2020. This means that younger people have shown the same propensity to switch jobs over the past 40 years, and older people have shown the same much lower job-switching rate. In both age ranges, people have been quite consistent over time.

Trust also is built from giving people the opportunity to learn in their jobs. If a person feels that her employer cares enough to provide access to educational alternatives such as training programs, outside university studies and/or just learning on the job, this tends to make the person feel more committed to the organization and in that sense more trusting of the environment. This trust is not necessarily embodied in one person, but rather it extends to the overall organization. Even so, the boss is the one who likely informs people about the educational opportunities and supports those activities, so that is where the trust-building starts.

Communicate effectively and be consistent; listen!

How often have you told other people to listen before they speak – and then failed to recognize that you make the same mistake? You can really generate buy-in from people if you listen to them and respond thoughtfully to their ideas, even if you don't agree with them. The opportunity to be heard counts for a lot, and being a good listener can help to generate trust with employees. This is not as simple to do as it may sound, since the boss is supposed to lead and to identify the way forward – and it is often difficult to stop and listen before pronouncing your great ideas.

Communication is like implementation. It is the last step in rolling out a strategy, and by the time you get to that stage you are tired of working on it, and you may pay inadequate attention to the importance of this step. When it comes to deadlines, you are much better served by announcing the deadline once, perhaps in writing through an email message, and then subsequently repeating the message in person in a meeting, and maybe even using a follow-up email as the deadline approaches. If the deadline is not on the same day, then people will run into other concerns that lead them to forget about the work deadline unless reminded.

In teaching we say that an effective method to get a point across is to tell the group (of students or executives) what you are going to explain to them; then explain it to them; and finally tell them what you have just explained. This three-barreled approach aims to cement the idea in firmly, whether the person listened carefully the whole time or even if their mind wandered a bit along the way.

Communication is more than just getting the message out. It is getting the message received and processed by the recipient. So, if you are trying to get your team to make a greater effort in building customer relationships, you need to not only state this, but also try to get individuals to think about exactly how they will do it. Having a meeting to discuss the ways in which you want to build better customer relations can help everyone, since surely ideas that you have not thought about will occur to someone else, and can be shared.

The point of this discussion about communication is to make sure that employees understand what you want from them, and how the organization supports them for achieving the goals. This should help to build trust in the people that the company has a clear direction for them to participate in, and that the rules of the game are clear for determining their performance. That is, if the message is about a work deadline, then that deadline should be clear, the way that the employee is expected to meet that deadline should be clear, and it should not be changed repeatedly along the way. As the wealth management executive said about his direct reports at the firm in Europe, they want to have clear statements of what is expected and when, so that they are not surprised in subsequent performance evaluations if they did not meet the targets. This was certainly true of my experience at the bank in South Africa. People just want a clear reading of what is expected of them, so that they can comfortably aim to achieve those goals. Setting goals in this way creates an environment in which people trust the organization, or the boss, not to pull unstated demands out of the hat at any point and to hold them responsible for something that is not manageable or reasonable.

Take responsibility for failures

I have never had a problem with taking responsibility for my division's failure to meet a goal or to carry out some task that was assigned. Whether it was my fault or not, as the leader I felt responsible for the team's performance. I say this because I expect that 100% of others in such positions feel the same way. If my subordinate messes up, I want to hold him responsible, but as far as the performance of my team is concerned, it is my responsibility, and I do not point fingers at whoever might have been the guilty party for missing some goal. Actually, I can easily imagine some leader getting frustrated and putting the blame on the subordinate who failed – but this is not useful behavior, and it certainly does not help build trust among the team members.

If you think of topsy-turvy times like under Covid-19, there have been so many disruptions to business that almost any company division has probably missed deadlines or output targets. This may be due to the inability of suppliers to get inputs to you on time, or due to lack of customers in retail businesses closed or partially closed by the quarantines and lockdowns used to deal with the virus. These chaotic conditions make it more important than ever for a boss to demonstrate her willingness to take responsibility for the team's achievements (or lack of them). People have been grasping for solid foundations in a world gone crazy, and a boss who can act in a stable and supportive manner can generate a huge amount of trust in the organization. This does not mean that the boss has a better understanding of the pandemic than everyone else, but that the boss can think clearly about the challenges and provide support to the team members who are looking for guidance.

Build trust gradually

It may seem obvious, but you cannot build trust in an instant. It takes some amount of time for people to observe trustworthy behavior, to see it repeated or continued and then to develop a feeling that the person or organization is trustworthy. When you come into an organization as a new leader, the first thing that people will do is look for your weaknesses. If you don't demonstrate credible and trustworthy behavior, you will create obstacles for your own ability to lead.

One of the simple things that new leaders often do is to spend time with each of her direct reports, and subsequently with people at least another level down in the organization. This process of getting to know each other is fundamental to building trust, and it requires many hours of meeting with these people over probably at least weeks or months once the new boss arrives. By meeting with each of the people on your team, you build up knowledge of their interests and concerns, and they learn similarly about you. You also build up knowledge about strengths and weaknesses of the organization, as perceived by these people. The value of such meetings goes far beyond building trust, and extends to building knowledge of the organization and of how people interact with each other and with the boss.

The key point here is that trust does not just happen from one statement or meeting when a new person enters the organization, as either the boss or as a manager/executive within it. It is not that you have to build up trust through major, highly-visible demonstrations of trustworthy behavior, but just that you need to be consistent in showing credible (honest, committed, collegial) behavior, and it has to grow on people. It may feel frustrating that you cannot instantly establish that feeling in people – but it does take time for the perceptions to be made and internalized by the members of the organization.

Stress is lower in high-trust organizations

An interesting finding in some academic research is that stress is lower in high-trust organizations. High-trust organizations include such companies as Google, Wegman's supermarkets and Genentech. Low-trust organizations include companies where bureaucracy prevails, where employees are not trusted to manage their tools or equipment without supervision and ones where people are discouraged from suggesting new ideas or better ways of doing things to their boss. Examples are hard to come by, because, among other things, such companies would probably sue the author and publication for slanderous statements, even if they are true!

Building business relationships requires trust: how do you get there?

Building relationships with suppliers and customers is also a challenge that requires trust-creation. Just as with employees, an individual from one company needs to demonstrate trustworthy behavior to gain the trust of the counterparty. In this case the person may be able to benefit from an existing relationship between the two organizations where trust already exists. Assuming that an existing relationship does not exist, the ways to create trust between the organizations is reasonably similar to that within an organization. That is, you need to demonstrate trustworthy behavior, such as presenting factual statements about your company's products or services, delivering as promised, and generally demonstrating credible behavior. In this case you would worry about trust in the other direction as well: can you trust the counterparty to deliver as agreed?

Even with the transactional nature of this relationship, that is, the fact that the relationship depends on transactions between the companies, the relations are still carried out by people, so personal relations are once again key. Maybe you cannot do team-building exercises with the other company, or offer job incentives for performance, but the rest of the ideas discussed above for building trust between people can largely be used in this inter-company context as well.

If an existing relationship does exist between the companies, then presumably trust is already there – although there certainly may have been mishaps in the past that tested the relationship. In any event, if the organizations have been working together for a while, there will be people who know each other between the two and they will have some level of trust already established. People may change jobs over time, and new people will appear in the relationship, but the historical trust generally will continue until someone or some event causes it to be lost. This could be anything from a company bankruptcy to a pandemic that changes the whole market. This is a powerful element of trust, i.e., that once established between two organizations, it is relatively easy to maintain trust unless someone or some event causes a drastic change in the relationship.

Notes

1   The William Tell story is a wonderful tale of courage and commitment, which led to the founding of Switzerland and its escape from the Habsburg empire. Even if the story is a myth, it certainly demonstrates a huge amount of trust – in himself and by his son – for William Tell back in 1291. After his feat, William Tell supposedly assassinated the Habsburg governor of his canton who had forced him to shoot the arrow at the apple on his son's head, and then he rallied other local farmers to start a new grouping of towns that eventually became Switzerland.
2   This was due to the fact that our university very quickly and effectively moved instruction online through Zoom, and students not only stayed with us, but new students joined our university from others that were not able to respond as quickly and successfully."
3   See Gallup Employee Engagement Survey, www.gallup.com/access/239210/gallup-q12-employee-engagement-survey.aspx

References

Goler, Lori, Janelle Gale, Brynn Harrington, and Adam Grant, 2018. The 3 Things Employees want: Career, Community, Cause. Harvard Business Review. (February 20). https://hbr.org/2018/02/people-want-3-things-from-work-but-most-companies-are-built-around-only-one

Marketwatch, 2020. "COVID-19 hit the hotel industry hard. Here's how hotels are pivoting in the new reality". www.marketwatch.com/story/covid-19-tur ned-the-hotel-industry-upside-down-but-it-wont-change-what-people-want-2020-08-23

Packard, David, 1995. *The HP-Way: How Bill Hewlett and I Built Our Company*. New York: Harper Collins Publishers.

Parker, Sharon K., Caroline Knight, and Anita Keller, 2020. Remote managers are having trust issues. *Harvard Business Review* (digital article). July 30.

Zak, Paul, 2017. The neuroscience of trust. *Harvard Business Review*. January–February. 3–8.

Chapter 5

Respect and self-esteem

Respect

Respect for a person is a key element of the work environment. If a person feels that the boss or the organization does not respect her as a member of the team, then it may be difficult for that person to be committed to the organization rather than feeling marginalized. This has nothing to do with performance, but rather with basic human expectations. Groucho Marx may have said that "I don't want to belong to any club that would accept me as one of its members", but most people do like to feel that others in an organization accept them. For any organization to accomplish anything, it has to convince the people within it that they matter and that the organization cares about them. In some organizations there may be a major emphasis on individual performance, which differentiates people from each other, but there still needs to be a basic human characteristic that is valued in everyone as well.

This kind of respect of one human being for another is sometimes called 'respect for persons' (Cranor 1975) or 'owed respect' (Rogers 2018), which is owed to everyone as a person regardless of their specific skills or qualities or performance. It might also be called personal respect, given that it relates to individual people in the context where all are equally valued as individuals, male or female, white or black, Chinese or French and so forth. This kind of respect requires people to accept the differences in other people, from physical characteristics to religion to nationality. In the context of a business, this kind of respect calls for creating a comforting or non-hostile work environment in the organization, where different people can all feel unthreatened and accepted.

A very different kind of respect is earned by a person based on some kind of performance measure. This could be respect earned by a baseball player for the demonstrated skill that got him to the major leagues, or by a musician who plays in a leading orchestra or by an architect who designs houses or office buildings. Within a business context this performance-related respect

DOI: 10.4324/9781003367512-5

could be for someone's ability to sell the company's services more success-fully than others, or someone's analytical ability to solve logistical problems or to create software for the company's use. In all of these instances people are differentiated from each other based on some kind of performance measure. This is not a cultural or religious difference, but some activity where the person's skill or ability is recognized.

There are other classifications of respect that do not fit into either of these two categories. For example, there is respect within a hierarchy for someone in a higher position. You may like or dislike the person, or her skills, but because she is the manager and you are the assistant manager, there has to be some respect for the position of the manager. Langdon (2007) called this 'social power'. It might also be seen as respect for the position, rather than for a particular person.

Another type of respect has to do with social norms. This certainly differs across societies, but the idea is common across them: showing respect is the proper way to act according to the society's normative and implicit rules. For example, in many societies it is seen as appropriate to show respect for elders, typically by treating them kindly and sometimes by giving them gifts or spe-cial treatment in public. So, this type of respect for elders does not have to do with any qualities of the elderly people, but just for their age. (Of course, it might be assumed that elders possess valuable knowledge that they could share, or that they are weak and deserve some support from others to help them, thus justifying the respect for either of these reasons.)

There is also respect for a person within the organization which implies that the organization cares about the person. This caring may be embodied in such policies as maternity leave, vacation days, health clinic availability and other services that support employees as people. It is a kind of communal respect, which is offered by the organization to its employees, rather than respect shown by one person for another. All of these additional facets of respect call for treating people fairly and equally, and according to the par-ticular society's norms.

Personal ('owed') respect

This may be one of the most important issues in organizations today, that is, demonstrating that people with different characteristics (e.g., race, sex, nationality) receive the same respect from bosses, from co-workers and from the organization more generally. This has become much more complicated with the populist governments elected in a number of countries in the 2010s, where anti-foreign and mean-spirited invective became acceptable for government leaders at the same time as legal protections for minorities and under-represented people such as women, blacks, Hispanics and to some extent Asians continued to grow in the United States.

This inconsistent way of doing things makes it quite complicated for companies to set policy that protects relevant groups while not being attacked by populists at the same time. It brings to mind companies such as Facebook and Google that purposefully try to build accepting and positive work environments at the same time as they are criticized by populists for bowing to left-wing pressures or failing to defend national security interests.

How much respect is really due to people just for showing up? I think that a lot is actually due to them, especially given that the people *are* the organization. If you cannot offer an environment that is attractive for employees to be part of, then they will leave and you won't have a company. The attraction may be more about income than about how people are treated, but at the root of any organization is a unifying factor which is that the people choose to work there. And under the law of many if not most countries today, the equality of people as employees is enshrined as a requirement in various ways. You cannot pay some people income below the minimum wage. You cannot discriminate against people because of skin color or gender. You cannot force people to work beyond whatever number of hours is contractually specified (if the job is paid on an hourly basis). And many other rules exist in many countries to protect employees as human beings.

An important element of this personal respect was noted by a South African executive in a commercial services company. He said that:

> Respect, in my view, is always a 'two-way street'. If you want respect, you should show respect. The guiding principle for me in over 38 years of working is to "Treat people the way you would like to be treated". In my culture (of Indian origin) respect is always awarded to everyone as courtesy and more so toward folks that are older than you are. I guess it is way of granting older people the benefit of years of experience and wisdom, taught through the University of life. Respect is also earned, by doing an exceptional job, being diligent, leading by example and doing tasks that you require others to do. In essence you earn respect and create great camaraderie if you are in the "trenches" with the people you lead.

A construction equipment manufacturing executive identified several ways that his company shows respect for its people at all levels. "Our company is very flexible to meet employee occasional needs (e.g. to attend a funeral or to get medical treatment). We respect people by listening to what they want/need". He also noted that the feeling of respect comes from regular reinforcement about concern for employees. "We try to tell them every day that they are doing a good job. We get everybody pizza one day a month or so to recognize great work. And each year everybody gets a t-shirt". These small gestures build up a strong feeling that the company cares for and respects the employees. The specific gestures may work in one company and not in another, or in one country but not another – however the idea of the small gestures is universal, and it is up to the executive to figure out which gestures fit in the particular context.

Even if a company is a professional services firm, with highly specialized employees, it has to offer everyone, from maintenance staff to clerical staff to professionals, fair treatment according to both the law and to societal expectations. It doesn't matter if one person's salary is ten times that of some-body else's; they all are equal in the personal/owed sense of respect. This idea is enshrined in US law, under which all people are supposed to be treated equally. Reality may be a bit different, with richer people sometimes able to obtain preferential treatment in legal dealings for example, but the principle is clear, as is the intent of the law. In companies the principle is that everyone should be treated equally as a human being, even if they are treated differently in terms of salary, job perks and other aspects of the job due to skills or capabilities.

Performance ('earned') respect

Let's look next at performance-based respect. This is perhaps easiest to see in the context of sports or the performing arts. People celebrate, that is, respect, great players or great performers. Whether it is a movie actress or a tennis player, people generally respect the quality of that actor/player's perform-ance. In this context the respect also implies that the high level of skill is recognized, and the observer also knows or feels that he could not perform that role or that sport with the same skill. I could not play baseball as well as Bryce Harper or play soccer as well as Lionel Messi, no matter how hard or long I trained. And similarly, I could not sing as well as Placido Domingo or act as well as Tom Hanks, even if I spent ten years practicing. These per-formance capabilities are definitely respected – even if we may think that the individual has other traits that are not so attractive, such as drinking too much or being antisocial.

According to the oil and gas executive,

> Showing respect is treating people with integrity, dignity and as much transparency as you can. I have found that over-communicating, and spending additional time to give the high-level view of a situation has been valuable for people who have been siloed or haven't had the opportunity to understand where or how a given decision/action impacts the overall organization. Giving that additional visibility and background tends to earn people's respect because it helps them realize they are an integral part to the company (or if they are not integral, allows them to them to think about what they can do to become an important team member … it's like a basketball player realizing he's on

the bench because he's not making free throws; it becomes clear that if he practices and gets better at free throws, he'll be able to better help the team win).

Superior performance is not quite so hard to achieve in the context of organizations, as opposed to basketball teams. We celebrate people who exceed company goals in sales, or who bring in a new major client. We likewise may celebrate a person who gets tasks done well and quickly in comparison with the average for the company. These kinds of performance are not impossible for the rest of us to attain in most cases, but the person who does achieve such levels of superior performance gains respect (and often financial compensation). That respect may come from co-workers, and it also should come from the boss in terms of recognition and maybe rewards.

Earned respect is particularly difficult to deal with in many organizations, because it is difficult to identify the contribution of an individual to a team performance. If the company increases income by 10% this quarter, is it because one person did a better job in sales, or another person did a better job in financial management? Typically, we cannot separate out completely the acts or performance of a person from the rest of a team or from the overall company. Increased profits may come from higher sales, lower costs, some combination, or maybe just from raising prices. Earning respect in this context is more difficult than observing that a baseball player has a batting average of .275, or a basketball player scores 20 points per game or a painter sells a painting for $50,000. But better company performance certainly can be respected and praised by the firm's leaders through widespread bonus payments and also by the outside community through positive reports in the press about the company.

Respect for position

I find this to be a fascinating issue within organizations around the world. The expectations are so different from one culture to another as far as how to demonstrate respect for position is concerned. There is no question that people in higher levels of authority and responsibility receive some degree of respect – or at least their position does. The position-holder may not be all that respectable based on other criteria such as quality of work or being enjoyable to be around. Anyway, there is a general acceptance around the world that a person in a higher position in the organization should receive respect for being in that position.

The way that this respect is expressed in meetings or other gatherings of the company is strikingly different in different cultures. I found in Mexico that, even in a university, people including professors expected their bosses to assign tasks to them, and then the employee was expected to carry out those tasks. There might be grumbling at the water cooler about the work that was assigned, but the context said that the boss sets the goals and the team follows them. This is probably an overstatement, because in every country professors have a pretty significant degree of latitude in carrying out their duties, even though some rules such as not alienating students and publishing academic journal articles are common everywhere.

In South Africa at the bank, and at banks elsewhere that I am familiar with, the boss sets the goals and the team follows them. That is, the same practice or style holds in this African banking context as in the Mexican university context. When I tried to operate my division (of leadership development) at the bank on a more 'academic' basis, allowing my direct reports to participate in decision-making regularly, it was difficult to implement such a policy. While we said across the bank that we wanted people to think for themselves and to look for new or better ways to do things, the top-down style of managing the organization was hard to adjust. This tends to be true of commercial banks everywhere, and insurance companies as well, but even within our financial services group, in the more freewheeling investment bank the hierarchy was pretty rigid as far as decision processes are concerned.

Another perspective on this theme comes from a financial services executive who led businesses in Germany and the United States. He said that respect came from subordinates when he demonstrated his interest in their work and asked questions to understand it better. As a leader he feels that he needs to generate respect for his position by using that position to support and encourage the members of the team. It is a simple or at least simple-sounding idea, but a boss can create an environment of respect just by demonstrating respect for the troops, through things as easy as asking questions about what they are doing to solve a problem or deal with some aspect of the business. This is not an interrogation to judge performance, but rather an interaction so that the boss can understand the subordinate's thinking and business actions. Maybe this is not precisely respect for the boss's position, but respect is generated because the person in his position showed respect first.

An interesting view of respect for position was presented by the senior executive in a South African trading and services company. He pointed out that: acting with integrity and staying true to your word creates respect among your bosses, peers and subordinates. Again, leadership by example is critical. It is the opposite of "Do as I tell you, not as I do", which creates animosity and erodes building both respect and trust. To a certain extent, one would have respect for authority in terms of the positions that are held, but behavior is what drives sustainable and deep genuine respect. Initially one would respect a position automatically, but if the person in that position does not behave in a responsible, ethical and fair manner, the respect disappears quite quickly and is replaced by skepticism and animosity.

This style has everything to do with Hofstede's power distance dimension of culture.[1] In high-power distance cultures, such as Mexico or the Middle

East, a top-down management style is very common. Also, in a commercial bank or an insurance company, this same top-down style fits the culture of these kinds of organizations in any country. By contrast, in the United States or the United Kingdom, there is a much lower power distance in the culture, and much more participative decision-making is common in organizations in general. And in professional service firms such as management consultancies and advertising agencies, lower power distance is common in contrast to commercial banks or fast-food restaurants. Respect for the position of a boss exists in both kinds of culture, high- and low-power distance, but the way in which it is carried out is notably different.

This respect of position might well be noted in the early 21st century with the populist governments that have been elected in quite a few countries. Judging from the poor approval ratings of many presidents and prime ministers in countries that have moved toward populist leaders since 2000, one might argue that they are not respected. That may be true for the specific person – but not for the office. I dare say that people still respect the office of the president in Brazil or the office of Prime Minister in the United Kingdom, even if they strongly object to the person holding that office.

Respect following social norms

While social norms are different in different cultures and countries, the idea of respecting other people for following the society's norms for behavior is common. There is no doubt that people (tend to) respect religious leaders in most religions, because of the idea that the religious leader helps people understand or follow their God. Of course, there are corrupt and incompetent religious leaders, but the respect for this kind of person is widely held in many quite different cultures. The social norm is that religious leaders are committed to following the dictates of their God, and this is viewed as respectable behavior.

Social norms exist in all aspects of life, although some are embodied in laws while others are only informal practices. And even some laws are ignored by social practice. For example, how many people pay attention to speed limits while driving? Evidence from observing drivers on the road shows that many, probably the majority of people, drive somewhat above the speed limit. This may be 1 or 2 miles per hour (or kilometers per hour) above the speed limit – but it is still against the letter of the law. Social norm says that this is ok, even though very occasionally the police will enforce the limit closely, and violators will pay a fine.

Another quite interesting example in the 2020s is the recreational use of marijuana in the United States. The consumption of marijuana used to be prohibited, like alcohol under Prohibition in the 1920–1933 time period. Now both marijuana production and consumption are legally permitted in some US States and not others; and by national law they are prohibited.

What a legal mess! The result is that social norms generally support the view of 'live and let live', that is, to allow those who want to consume marijuana to do so. But this view is not held by everyone, and a substantial minority of Americans do not agree with it. The Pew Research Center (2019) found in a survey in 2019 that 59% of Americans support legal marijuana consumption, for recreational and medical purposes, and a Gallup poll (2020) in 2020 found that 68% of Americans favored it – in both cases somewhat more than half of the total sample of people who responded. The net result is that there is not a consistent social norm, and there is also not a consistent government policy.

A less controversial social norm is when respect is paid to people in the organization just for being fellow members of that organization. In small, entrepreneurial organizations, this is perhaps easier to understand, because people know each other and interact with each other daily. So, it is important to behave in a mutually supportive – or at least not antagonistic – way. This does not mean that everyone is best friends with everyone else, but rather that everyone understands that together they are the organization, and it is important to show respect for each other to make the environment a positive one to work in. This is harder to see in a large organization, except perhaps in the smaller teams of people who work together in a division or on a project.

Self-esteem

Another kind of respect is self-respect, or self-esteem. This is an interesting challenge for a company to deal with, since it is really in the domain of a person to achieve self-approval. Nevertheless, a company can provide conditions that support an individual's development of greater self-respect. The discussion here relates to the person's self-esteem within the context of an organization (Bowling et al. 2010), rather than self-esteem more broadly in other aspects of life (e.g., as a parent or a student). Even so we have to recognize that someone's self-esteem within a company also derives from their overall self-esteem, so the two ideas are not separable.

There is a difference between self-respect and self-esteem. Self-respect refers to the regard that an individual has for him/herself. This respect will then lead a person to act in ways that s/he views as having value. On the other hand, self-esteem refers to an appreciation that an individual has for that person's own abilities and skills. So, a writer will have self-esteem for being able to write poems or newspaper articles or books successfully, or an athlete will have self-esteem from the demonstrated ability to play a sport well. The intent within an organization is to develop an environment in which people can feel respected (and develop consequent self-respect) for their work and their commitment, and at the same time to develop an environment where people feel that their particular skills are valued and that reinforces their self-esteem.

The kinds of factor that contribute to self-esteem, and that are relevant in the organization setting, include: the person's general self-esteem separate from that related to the company; the positive features of the job environment, such as autonomy in the job, clear job definition, good management and organizational support; the negative features of the job environment, such as job instability, work overload and role ambiguity. The impact of greater self-esteem in the organizational setting should be: greater job satisfaction, better motivation and productivity, and even better health of the employee. The psychology literature includes a number of studies that find that greater self-esteem does indeed improve performance, but also other studies that show a lack of correlation between the two (Ferris et al. 2010).

There is some degree of bidirectional influence as well. Greater self-esteem may lead to better job performance, while better job performance may lead a person to feel greater self-esteem (e.g., Krauss and Orth 2021). This reciprocal effect, which has been shown empirically in a number of studies, simply means that a company seeking to improve job performance generally will have to take into account the responses of both low-self-esteem individuals and high-self-esteem individuals. A manager trying to motivate her subordinates needs to look for ways to deal with both types of people – though by rewarding superior job performance, she may be able to raise the self-esteem of those who start out lower on the scale.

Creating an environment to increase employee self-esteem

The steps that a manager or an organization can pursue to increase employees' self-esteem are largely the same as those used to motivate people to increase their performance. That is, creating an organizational environment that empowers people and makes them feel that the company cares about them also tend to help improve self-esteem.

The senior executive at the South African commercial services company pointed out that: "If you want to develop and encourage innovation, you should be able to accept that there will always be failures. It is part of the learning process. To ensure that people try continuously to improve themselves and the company's products and/or services, [they need to feel self-esteem. To accomplish this you need to] encourage people to take calculated risks, and when things don't work out, look for the positives and the learnings. Reprimanding employees for trying to do things differently and seeking to improve a company's offerings, will destroy self-esteem and often leads to employees taking the safe route and not trying to improve. They will stick to the tried and tested. This will stifle innovation and destroy motivation and inherently self-esteem. Recognition and feedback are key to building and maintain self-esteem. Self-esteem will drive self-confidence and promote a culture of excellence and pride."

The oil and gas executive said that:

> I try to help people develop higher self-esteem through skill expansion (training) or vocabulary (where they need to grow to become a better communicator). Most people see their path to grow (in terms of pay and job title), but greatly appreciate ways to accelerate that path. I've found that small bursts (10–15 minutes) of focused training tends to be the best way to grow people's self-esteem, even if you don't call it training. I will spend a few minutes in one-on-one discussions providing historical background on a technology, process, business relationship or project/program. The "give more background than you probably want to know" approach has worked well for me. I also pair up specialists who are very good at some things (i.e., financial models/Excel) that can help an underperformer figure out how to do something him/herself, and then require that they do it.

From my experience in South Africa at the bank, I found that especially with people who had faced many restrictions under the previous Apartheid regime, they really, really appreciated the opportunity to make decisions and have a degree of autonomy in their work, which demonstrated that our organization had trust in them. It was a superb way to build self-esteem among the managers in my team.

Conclusions

Both respect from others and self-esteem from themselves are desirable conditions to offer people in an organization. The discussion in this chapter points to a number of ways in which companies can try to achieve these outcomes.

First, on the subject of respect, we should differentiate between owed respect, which is owed to anyone as a person in the organization, and earned respect, which is given to individuals who demonstrate superior performance. Second, we should pursue behavior and policies that demonstrate respect for people in the organization for both owed and earned reasons.

As far as self-esteem is concerned, since greater self-esteem is associated with better performance, then an organization should try to help employees raise their level of self-esteem. At the same time, people start out with higher or lower levels of self-esteem, and the leaders in the organization need to know how to help drive good performance from both types of people.

Note

1 See any discussion of Hofstede's cultural dimensions. For example, Hofstede, Geert,1984. *Culture's Consequences: International Differences in Work-related Values*. Newbury Park, CA: Sage Publications. Or his website: https://geerthofst ede.com/

References

Bowling, Nathan, Kevin J. Eschleman, Qiang Wang, Cristina Kirkendall, and Gene Alarcon, 2010. A meta-analysis of the predictors and consequences of organization-based self-esteem. *Journal of Occupational and Organizational Psychology*, 83, 601–26.

Cranor, Carl, 1975. Toward a theory of respect for persons. *American Philosophical Quarterly*, 12(4) October, 309–19.

Ferris, Lance, Huiwen Lian, Douglas Brown, Fiona Pang, and Lisa Keeping, 2010. Self-esteem and job performance: The moderating role of self-esteem contingencies. *Personnel Psychology*, 63, 561–93.

Gallup, 2020. "Support for legal marijuana inches up to new high of 68%". November 9. https://news.gallup.com/poll/323582/support-legal-marijuana-inc hes–new-high.aspx

Hofstede, Geert, 1984. *Culture's Consequences: International Differences in Work-related Values*. Newbury Park: Sage Publications.

Krauss, Samantha, and Ulrich Orth, 2021. Work experiences and self-esteem development: A meta-analysis of longitudinal studies. *European Journal of Personality*, 36(6),1–21.

Langdon, Susan, 2007. Conceptualizations of respect: Qualitative and quantitative evidence of four (five) themes. *Journal of Psychology*, 141(5), 469–84.

Pew Research Center, 2019. "Two-thirds of Americans support marijuana legalization". November 14. www.pewresearch.org/fact-tank/2019/11/14/americans-support-marijuana-legalization/

Rogers, Kristie, 2018. Do your employees feel respected? *Harvard Business Review*. July–August. 2–11.

Chapter 6

Fairness

Three broad areas of fairness in business

There are three broad headings under which fairness in business can be categorized. First, *process* or *procedural* fairness exists when decisions are made in the organization in a transparent manner, applying the same procedures and criteria to everyone, so that employees understand how those decisions are being made.[1] Second, *outcome* or *distributive* fairness exists when people in like circumstances are treated equally – and this result is evident to employees, so they can see the fairness in action. Third, *approach* or *goal* fairness exists when the organization conveys clearly to employees the goals being pursued, so that employees know how their work lines up with those goals, and their performance can be evaluated in that light.

Why does fairness matter? In a sense you could argue that fairness is a quality that underpins the market economic system. Businesspeople expect to receive transparent and accurate information about products and services from their suppliers and their customers, so that they can pursue purchases and sales in good faith. If you could not trust your suppliers to deliver the items you contract to buy as agreed, then the whole system would be undermined. In another sense fairness matters because it is an expectation of the society. Business has a 'license to operate' if it operates fairly and by the rules, without cheating people or other businesses. If a company cannot be trusted to operate legally and fairly, it ultimately won't be allowed to operate at all, either by legal decree or by customers and suppliers rejecting it.

Let's look at each of the three aspects of fairness in turn.

Process/procedural fairness

Process fairness is in the eye of the beholder, that is, the employee. The drivers of process fairness, according to Brockner (2006) are three things: how much input employees believe they have in decision-making; how employees believe that decisions are made and carried out; and how managers behave

DOI: 10.4324/9781003367512-6

in explaining things to employees (Brockner 2006, p.2). Note that process fairness does not talk about the outcome of decisions in the organization, but rather it talks about how decisions are perceived to be made.

This kind of fairness can easiest be seen in the context of decisions within an organization about who gets promoted (and who does not), or who gets laid off and who does not. When one employee can see how another is treated by the boss or by the company, this evidence is quickly assimilated and judged as fair or unfair. If my performance is superior to that of a colleague in my same job category, yet she gets a promotion and I do not, this sends a clear signal of unfairness.

If layoffs are needed, for example due to reduced demand for the company's services during the Covid-19 pandemic, every employee wanted to know what criteria were being used to decide who stays and who goes. Remember in the United States during the early days of the pandemic, when 'essential' workers were allowed to continue working, where everyone else was deemed to be subject to at least temporary layoff during the economic downturn? And the essential workers were assigned to two categories, 1a and 1b, for access to the vaccines that were being developed for Covid-19. Question: Were those criteria fair? It is difficult to say, but happily [i]n most situations, the drastic conditions of the Covid-19 pandemic do not apply, so that layoffs are due to more mundane factors such as reduced sales in a company that does not see a solution to fix that problem, or mechanization of a process that was formerly done primarily by people.

It is not that hard to achieve process fairness in these contexts, as long as the company is willing and able to state the decision-making criteria clearly and demonstrate that they are applied evenhandedly to the employees involved in the decision. In the case of a job promotion, especially in professional services organizations such as consulting firms, law firms and investment banks, it is often the case that three or four people at one level demonstrate good performance, but the next rung on the ladder is not wide enough to accommodate all of them. If you work at McKinsey or Goldman Sachs or Kirkland & Ellis as a junior member of the professional team, you know that the odds on progressing to partner are not high. Even if you put in superhuman effort, you may not be promoted when that time comes. So, what you want to see are transparent criteria for the decision and hopefully some differentiation of the work done by your colleague who may get promoted ahead of you. This may not be easy to distinguish, so it is up to the employer to try to provide guidance to the employee about how the decision was made. I have seen good people pushed out of these organizations, as well as from leading business schools and other organizations, when their performance was very good, but the number of positions at the next level (or with tenure at a university) was limited, so that cuts had to be made somehow.

The selections that I have had to make, as a bank executive and as a business school dean, were never tremendously difficult when one person had to be compared with another. I never found that 'everything else was equal' in making a promotion decision, but rather that somebody did have identifiable superior performance results. Where I ran into this fairness issue was in hiring decisions. Due particularly to equal opportunity laws, I had to search out minorities and women to employ. When looking at resumes rather than at performance within my organization, it often was the case that resumes looked fairly similar, and that choosing a minority or a woman was possible. But you could not say that 'everything else was equal', because the minority candidates and women generally tended to have had fewer previous opportunities to demonstrate their capabilities. So, they looked weaker on that criterion.

An executive in a construction equipment manufacturing company said that: "It is not so hard to decide on promotions, because there are few people in teams. When somebody retires, he is replaced by the next person in seniority". This was relatively easy to manage in this company, because people who stayed with the firm over the years had to demonstrate good performance. So, it was not like two people would be competing for the same job when a person retired.

He also noted that:

> "We hate to get rid of people". [If someone is not performing as well as we think should be the case,] we find ways to reassign them – unless someone is stealing from the company. We hire people for 90–180 days from a temp agency, and then decide whether to keep them or not at the end of that period.

Once someone passes that 180-day trial period, he/she becomes part of the team and is supported to ensure their successful performance.

While the principle of making such hiring decisions based on criteria other than performance is understandable, it is not easy to do. Legal mandates made it easier to accept but still hard to rationalize. What I found as a result of making such decisions is that the people selected due partially to race or gender actually turned out (generally) to have equally good or bad performance once they joined my organization as people with greater previous experience. That is, the women performed on average just as well as the men, and the previously disadvantaged groups in South Africa performed in the bank just as well as those who had experienced better education and better opportunities under the earlier Apartheid regime that lasted until 1994. Very interesting! The outcome with respect to performance of women has been well-documented: not only do women tend to perform as well as men in organizations, but more women in leadership of companies produces *better* company performance (e.g., Goldman Sachs 2020; Noland et al. 2016).

With all of this said, it is still often difficult to make promotion or layoff decisions. Just think of the early days of the Covid-19 pandemic, when many if not most businesses faced reduced demand for their products or services. How does an organization decide who to keep and who to let go when sales drop through the floor (separate from the 'essential workers' categories)? If I operate a hotel, then I would like to keep the 'best' people. But when almost no one was traveling in 2020, how far could a hotel company go in maintaining staff? We knew that hotel rooms would eventually be used again, but even today in 2022 the amount of business travel remains much lower than pre-pandemic. So, again, who can you keep, and who needs to be dropped?

Fairness in this context is difficult to demonstrate. The hotel operating company may decide to keep all managers and lay off all staff involved in cleaning, restaurant operations and various guest services. That would avoid the appearance of unfairness, but it would almost assuredly cause the best-performing staff members to find jobs elsewhere and then not be willing to return when travel and hotel use recuperate from the pandemic. If the hotel company were to try to keep only the 'best' staff performers employed, then it would probably be difficult to decide where to draw the line, and even so, everyone in a staff position would realize the frailty of the company's commitment to them, and might go looking for another job anyway. There is not much that is easy when dealing with a pandemic!

Some partial solutions were chosen by organizations. Having people temporarily work fewer hours per week (usually for the corresponding lower pay) at least reduced the costs to the company, even though losses still occurred. The expectation was that the pandemic would eventually end, and that people could return to pre-pandemic working conditions, so that keeping people in the organization was better than just letting them go. In other cases people were put on forced furlough (unpaid or partially paid vacation) for a period of months, since their work was not needed. The challenge here of course is that no one knew how long the pandemic conditions would remain, so the length of the furlough had to be either extended, or people eventually laid off, or the crisis had to abate so the furloughs would no longer be necessary. Fortunately in the United States, government policies were implemented to subsidize the companies that were hurt by the pandemic, so that they could survive the downturn in demand for their products and services, and it was only after more than a year that the subsidies were phased out. The government budget cost was enormous, but the avoidance of massive bankruptcies was worth it.

Let's move away from the pandemic and talk about 'normal' times. Consider fairness in evaluating performance the way that Jack Welch legendarily ran General Electric (GE) Corporation during 1981–2001. His demand was that each division had to evaluate performance of individual employees on an annual basis, and the lowest-rated 10% of the distribution of employees would be let go each year.[2] This policy was clear, and the criteria were only imprecise because the manager had to assign performance evaluations for each person, and those evaluations were not necessarily 100% transparent. Even so, this policy is very clear, and people who were let go did understand the logic, even if they disagreed with the results. I think that today people would shudder at this kind of policy, which demonstrates no human empathy or regard for employees' feelings. It nevertheless achieved the goal of providing a strong incentive for employees to perform well, and it also achieved the goal of letting go some people who managers had empathy for but whose performance they could not defend.

Procedural fairness was seen by a senior executive in a management consulting firm as relating mainly to job assignments (staffing decisions). He noted that the Big 3 firms all have to deal with this main fairness issue. Promotions and bonuses are also issues, but the rules are clear for these decisions, and so they are not subject to much contention. Staffing decisions for client projects are difficult, because there are a finite number of client projects at any given time, and consultants have to be assigned to the teams. People at different levels and with different backgrounds have to been fit together into a good project team each time, and this is not an easy or particularly transparent task. At a given time, there will be some consultants not assigned to a project, after a previous one finished, and the tension is for the consultants to get assigned to interesting and important projects.

Another executive from a financial services organization with experience in the United States and the Middle East said that:

> Fairness is not an organizational value that happens on its own; fairness occurs when the executive team is intentional. If employees perceive the company is not fair, they will be immediately demotivated and will soon lose interest and passion. One of the best descriptions of a former CEO and colleague of mine was that "he is prickly, but fair." We knew he would speak his mind, he could be extremely tough, but we always knew he would be fair and act with integrity. While employees may not have been comfortable, they always knew he was fair. As a result, the employees were motivated with his candor and fairness.

An important issue noted by one analyst (Hancock et al. 2018) is that performance metrics as established in an MBO (management by objectives) statement at the beginning of the year may need to be changed during the course of the year, as conditions change. Many organizations have a goal-setting point at the beginning of the performance year, and then jump to the end of the year to judge results. If you don't take into account the changes in your business, the regulatory environment, competitor moves and so forth during the year, then goals set for individuals at the beginning of the year may not correspond to what will actually be expected at the end of the year. Some flexibility is needed to adjust goals in mid-stream, to account for possible changes in key conditions.

Looking at fairness in a broader context, away from hiring and firing decisions, a senior executive in a South African commercial services company pointed out that:

> Fairness is often driven by perception; and a lack of understanding of decision making and can lead to employees feeling disillusioned and feeling unfairly treated. It is therefore very important to ensure that decisions involving or affecting groups of employees are well articulated and clearly communicated with a focus on minimizing ambiguity.
>
> Whether you are dealing with different generations of people or not, it is critical for you as a leader to understand clearly what makes your individual direct reports tick. You cannot manage everyone the same, because people have different aspirations and ambitions and as such will allocate different importance to things. The trick is to find these touchpoints and manage accordingly. A one-brush approach can often be dangerous. This is not to be confused with consistency of decision making.

Outcome fairness

Whether or not the process through which a decision is made is fair, the outcome of the decision is a separate issue. The process may be deemed as fair, but the outcome not fair at all. An example created by Kahneman et al. (1986) was the change in price of snow shovels charged by a hardware store after a big snowstorm. They asked survey respondents if it would be fair for the store to raise snow shovel prices after the storm to ration the limited supply of available shovels (from $15 to $20). Of the respondents 82% said 'no', the store should not be allowed to gouge consumers for $5 additional profit, resulting in a $5 loss to the consumers. While it was not presented in the example, another mechanism would have been to simply sell the snow shovels at the existing price to whoever arrived at the store earliest, until they ran out. Or perhaps having an auction for snow shovels and letting the market determine the price. Outcome fairness based on the experiment seems to have required the store not to profit from consumers just due to the random weather phenomenon rather than from any new value added by the store. So, the only fair outcome would have been to sell the snow shovels at the existing price until they ran out.

Kahneman et al. concluded that "The cardinal rule of fair behavior is surely that one person should not achieve a gain by simply imposing an equivalent loss on another" (p.731). This is certainly one clear lesson from the issue of outcome fairness.

This example reminds me of the situation after Hurricane Andrew in Miami, when about 25,000 houses were destroyed by the wind and water. Home Depot was swamped by demand for plywood and other home repair materials, and they strategically chose not to raise prices significantly, but to serve the community as well as they could, and to bring in additional wood and other supplies from their warehouses elsewhere in the country. This did not solve the huge extra demand for materials that occurred, as the company did run out of materials repeatedly over the subsequent months. However, it was seen as a very fair outcome, and Home Depot received outstanding community regard for a long time based on their actions (Lohr 1992).

As far as dealing with employees is concerned, outcome fairness can be observed in many ways. For example, in assigning pay increases in a public-sector organization, it is often possible for the employees to see their own raises as well as those of their colleagues. This is about as transparent of a situation as you can imagine, and it leads to almost guaranteed grumbling among the team members. "I did most of the work on our key project, and he got a higher raise than I did". "How could you (the boss) give her such a big raise and only give more valuable contributors half that?" I don't know how to escape this sniping completely, because people are blinded by their own limited knowledge of the situation, where the boss has much more information about everyone's activities and results. Nevertheless, this problem arises in many organizations that are required to make compensation information public.

I found that giving very similar percentage raises to most people, and only separating out a few high-performers and low-performers whose work could clearly be identified as such worked pretty well. In the corporate context, bonuses could also be used to reward people more or less than the average – and in some cases the bonus information is not available to public scrutiny. A real problem for me was that in one instance in the Middle East I had a fantastic performer in one division (finance) whose performance was clearly extraordinary, and another fantastic performer (in marketing) who likewise had brilliant performance for the year. They were the best of all performers in my division of about 80 professionals. I gave both of them the same percentage raise, notably above the average. The finance person was extremely upset because her performance had been the best of her career, and she only got a performance benefit equal to that of another person, whose work she valued less. You can see the basically unwinnable situation for me, and so I responded by offering perks such as travel opportunities and involvement in decision-making that I thought were reasonable (fair!). But I am not sure that she ever forgave me for the perceived slight in relative compensation.

An oil and gas industry executive said that:

> [outcome] Fairness is where the coach puts the best players in the game to put the team in the best position to win. Each player is treated with respect and dignity, however not everybody is treated equally. Specifically,

some people's abilities, relationships, or emotional awareness warrant giving them higher impact/value/pay roles or more playing time (or time in front of the customer, or leadership of a team). If someone can create more value for the team, I am willing to promote them or pay them more relative to the next person. Initiative (and notably doing things beyond their paygrade) is the top value creator from what I've seen in my work experiences. Demonstrating fairness is something that shows up in results from decisions, it's not something that I have spent much time trying to justify to others. On the flipside, when I have had to fire people or lay people off it has been because there has been inferior effort or results from those people, and there was no surprise that they were being let go.

What about the situation in a multinational company where people in one country are paid differently than people doing the same job in another country? For example, pay to a supervisor or a technician in the United States versus pay to someone doing that same job in the Indian subsidiary of that same US company. Obviously, incomes are much lower in India than in the United States. But within the same company for the same job? The answer to this question may appear simple to many people. You pay in Rome what the Romans earn. Or, in this case, you pay Indian salaries in India. Not so fast. If you want to keep excellent people, you will probably have to offer more than the competitors in your target country. If you want to transfer people from India to the US home office or to some other foreign affiliate, your company will need to have a 'fair' salary structure. This subject is probably too complex for the current discussion, but suffice it to say that you can put together compensation packages that reflect local conditions and adjustments for home-office treatment of employees as far as human resources issues are concerned.

The senior executive in the management consulting firm said that there are definitely different salaries in different countries, and that his firm tries to offer competitive salaries within the national context. If a consultant is transferred into a different country, then salary has to be adjusted accordingly. Even so, someone from the US home office getting assigned to work medium-term in an emerging market will still receive a salary increment above local conditions to reflect his/her base country.

One of the consumer products executives said that, in India, for example, the pay scale for local managers and executives was similar to what competitors pay, including perks such as a driver and an assistant for higher-level executives. In addition, a small number of 'global executives' were assigned to the Indian subsidiary, and they were paid on a global salary basis, applied to whatever country these people were assigned to. Some of them were from India, others from the United States, United Kingdom and elsewhere. The global cohort were few in number and generally were assigned to different countries every few years.

Approach or goal fairness

A very interesting challenge today is to identify what the actual purpose of the organization is. We cannot blithely say that 'maximizing shareholders' wealth' is the goal, as much as finance might want to assert this target. Today in the auto industry, for example, there is enormous pressure on automakers to reduce the environmental damage caused by vehicle emissions. So, many companies are pursuing electric (battery-powered) vehicles, and others are exploring hydrogen fuel cells, as well as some other alternatives. The point is that an auto company today has to deal with both competition from other gasoline-powered (and diesel-powered) vehicle producers and competition from the alternative-energy vehicles, particularly electric cars produced by Tesla and others. People who work in an auto company need to understand that the traditional assembly lines, supply chains and distribution channels may change due to the switch to alternative fuels

Many if not most other industries face nontraditional challenges related to environmental protection, women's and minority rights, and other issues that might be grouped under the heading of ESG (environmental, social and governance) criteria. These issues have become much more important as Millennials and Gen Z investors grow in numbers and in wealth relative to earlier generations. These investors are paying more attention to ESG activities of companies, and so alternative or additional goals are now frequently being pursued by publicly traded companies.

The executive from management consulting said that Millennials and Gen Z consultants in his firm did not have any different perceptions of fairness than their older counterparts – but these younger groups are pushing for the firm to get more involved in global social issues such as pursuing the UN's Sustainable Development Goals. So far, in any event, the firm has not taken up any of these issues!

On this theme, the executive from financial services now working for a family conglomerate said that:

> Demonstrating fairness begins with integrity; a fair company is committed to doing the right things, irrespective of circumstances. But that is not enough; a company must be transparent about what they do and why. Fairness and transparency go together; you cannot do one without the other. If employees know that the company is transparent and fair, and if they are disappointed in being passed over for a promotion, they are less likely to quit or become permanently demotivated. While this is a fundamental principle for young and seasoned employees alike, Millennials or Gen Z people require transparency and fairness or they quit; they do not suffer a corporate bureaucracy that treats them in a way that is perceived as demeaning or degrading.

So, there is in this case a notable distinction between how older people react to issues of fairness versus the younger generations today.

Implementation of a fair evaluation process

The key to having a fair evaluation process is not necessarily the process itself but rather the *perception* that the process is fair. For example, according to Hancock et al. (2018) there are three elements that matter most in employee perceptions of fairness in performance management. They are:

1 Linking business performance goals to business priorities
2 Getting managers to coach their employees
3 Differentiating compensation to reflect different performance

1. In the first instance it is possible for some jobs to be linked to business priorities such as hiring people from disadvantaged groups or treating subordinates fairly. But for line workers who do not make hire/fire decisions or deal with subordinates, the job evaluation cannot be linked to those ESG concerns. This does not disallow the broader criteria to be used for some people in the company, just not for everyone.

    For me at the bank in South Africa it was easy to use equal opportunity criteria in hiring people in my division. The national labor law required hiring preference to be given to previously disadvantaged groups, so that our employee profile would meet minimum percentages of non-white people at different levels of the organization. This was mainly for junior managers, senior managers and executives.
2. Getting managers to coach their subordinates toward better performance sounds like a very logical and sensible policy. The challenge is that many managers are not good coaches; coaching is a skill that needs to be developed. So, the organization can invest in some training of managers to do the coaching that is needed. This may not solve the problem completely, but it is a step in the right direction for sure.
3. Differentiating compensation to reflect different performance can be a challenge as I pointed out above in my Middle East example. You can offer great salary increases to people who perform better, but if salaries are known to everyone, then you cannot avoid the criticisms that will come from people who feel unfairly compensated relative to a co-worker. I think that the answer here is that you should do the salary differentiation based on performance, and then have thick skin to deal with the criticisms that will undoubtedly arise.

Views of fairness across countries

As you can see from the examples of executives in different countries and in different industries, fairness is not different as a concept anywhere. Even so, specific treatment such as compensation definitely differs from one country to another, based at a minimum on personal income levels that differ greatly across countries. And if your company is multinational, then compensation to people assigned to overseas positions has to reflect both the local conditions in that country as well as compensation levels in the home country. In this context, expatriates are typically paid either according to home country salaries plus additional compensation for the overseas 'hardships' such as payment for kids in school and/or for maintaining a house at home as well as one in the other country and so forth – or they may be paid on the host-country salary scale, plus the added benefits needed to compensate for additional costs of maintaining a home in both countries.

The examples here and in other studies (e.g., Yeoman and Mueller 2016; Hancock et al. 2018) show that fairness is perceived similarly by people from different cultures. If one person in the organization is given an opportunity to participate in a skill-building seminar or course, then others at the same level in the organization are going to expect to be treated similarly. This is just as true in Mexico as it is in the United States or in Spain or South Africa. And people are more similar with respect to their expectations of procedural fairness (how decisions are made) than with respect to outcome fairness (how resources are allocated), since the available resources are different in different contexts.

Conclusions

In the context of their jobs, people everywhere expect to be treated fairly. There are several dimensions of fairness, which are not all equal across countries and cultures. For the most part, people expect to have clear rules about what their jobs entail and what behavior is appropriate. This procedural fairness is an expectation that exists everywhere. On the other hand, the outcomes of decision-making differ to some extent across cultures and countries, so fairness in things like compensation is not as easy to identify or achieve.

Goal or approach fairness has become more nuanced in the 21st century, as Millennials and Gen Z employees and executives look for their companies to pursue nontraditional goals such as providing equal opportunities to women or aiming for the company to reduce its carbon footprint (i.e., its contribution to global warming). When a company includes in its statement of principles or its mission some of the United Nations SDGs (sustainable development goals), then fairness implies rewarding individual activities that support the achievement of those goals. There is a long way to go to get from the slogans that have popped up to some kind of orderly way to measure achievement of these goals and to reward performance for such behavior. Even Google's statement "Don't be evil" is not particularly measurable – although it does clearly signify the company's intent. And Facebook's original slogan, "It's free and always will be" had a similar pro-equality and positive social impact intent, even though it also was difficult to measure.

Perhaps the single most important aspect of fairness is how it is perceived. No matter what system for decision-making or evaluation that may be used, or what rewards are offered for good performance, the critical element in all of this is how the employee/individual perceives the fairness of the process or the decision. A successful company needs to pay careful attention to getting that perception lined up with the company's intent, through communication with employees, through training of managers and executives about how to coach their people and through maintaining a consistent process that rewards superior performance.

Notes

1   In principle, transparency is clear. In fact, people often need to have the reward criteria or conditions re-explained to them so that they feel treated appropriately. It is easy to have clear rules, but not so easy to have employees recognize them. *Perception* of fairness is central in this regard.

2   Actually, his policy allowed for people in the bottom 10% of performers to spend one more year at GE to try to move themselves out of that category or to find another job. Even so, this is a pretty draconian policy. See Jack Welch (2005).

References

Brockner, Joel, 2006. Why it's so hard to be fair. *Harvard Business Review*, (March). 84(3).

Goldman Sachs, 2020. "Womenomics". *Global Strategy Paper #45*. October 13. 1–36. www.goldmansachs.com/insights/pages/womenomics-europe-moving-ahead.html

Hancock, Bryan, Elizabeth Hioe, and Bill Schaninger, 2018. "The fairness factor in performance management". *McKinsey Quarterly*. April. 1–10. www.mckinsey.com/business-functions/people-and-organizational-performance/our-insights/the-fairness-factor-in-performance-management

Kahneman, Daniel, Jack L. Knetsch, and Richard H. Thaler, 1986. Fairness as a constraint on profit seeking: Entitlements in the market. *The American Economic Review*, 76(4), 728–41.

Lohr, Steve, 1992. "Lessons from a hurricane: It pays not to gouge". *New York Times*, Late Edition (East Coast); New York, September 22, D.1. www.nytimes.com/1992/09/22/business/lessons-from-a-hurricane-it-pays-not-to-gouge.html

Noland, Marcus, Tyler Moran, and Barbara Kotschwar, 2016. "Is gender diversity profitable? Evidence from a global survey". *Peterson Institute for International Economics Working Paper 16-3*. February. 1–35. www.piie.com/publications/wp/wp16-3.pdf

Welch, J., 2005. Cruel and Darwinian? Try Fair and Effective. In *Winning*. Harper Business. New York. Ch. 3. pp. 37–52.

Yeoman, Ruth and Milena Mueller Santos, 2016. "Fairness and organizational performance". Briefing Number 3. Said Business School. (November 11). www.sbs.ox.ac.uk/sites/default/files/2018-06/fairness_and_organizational_performance_insights_for_supply_chain_management_mib_briefings_no_3_hf241116.pdf

Chapter 7

How important is integrity in business?

Introduction

We talk often about how integrity is important for a person in leading a company, so that subordinates can observe the leader's behavior and (hopefully) recognize it for being honest and sincere and based on solid moral values. The idea of running a business in an honest way, with integrity, seems like a good idea. Some questions are: Is this really an accurate statement, that integrity matters? How does integrity matter in dealing with subordinates (and people above you) in an organization? Do people view integrity differently in different countries or cultures?

While there certainly are differences about what people view as acceptable 'white lies' in different cultures, the fundamental expectation in organizations around the world is that bosses and employees will act in a truthful manner. That is, they will demonstrate integrity. In some countries it is considered reasonable to try to evade personal income taxes. In many if not most countries it is considered reasonable to drive your car (somewhat) faster than the speed limit. But in no context is it considered acceptable to steal from your employer, or to lie about work that you have done. The issue of integrity really is important in business, though its limits may be a bit fuzzy.

How do you define integrity?

A dictionary definition is: "adherence to moral and ethical principles; soundness of moral character; honesty" (from www.dictionary.com). A second definition from the same source is: "the state of being whole, entire, or undiminished". Of course, the first definition fits our context of human behavior better than the second, which relates more to political or governmental integrity (e.g., of geographic territory). And even the first definition leaves some room for complexity, since it seems to say that honesty is another word for integrity – but honesty does not necessarily mean adherence to moral principles. A person could easily be honest and admit that "I

DOI: 10.4324/9781003367512-7

killed Joe because I did not like him". That would not show much integrity, however! There has to be a moral basis that underlies integrity.

A more detailed definition offered by Becker (1998) is that: "integrity [is] … loyalty, in action, to rational principles (general truths) and values. … Integrity involves acting according to a code (integrated system) of morally justifiable principles and values". (pp.157–8) His view is consistent with that of Huberts (2018), who says that "integrity is seen as the quality of acting in accordance or harmony with relevant moral values, norms, and rules" (p.S20). These two definitions offer a little more substance for our use in considering integrity in business. They emphasize that integrity must involve actions, so that a person's actions can be seen as either demonstrating integrity or not. And those actions must follow values, or a system of morally justified principles. It is more than just honesty.

Integrity in business

Even with the above effort to be precise in defining integrity, a simple example in business that shows integrity is that we expect bosses and employees to be honest (truthful) in their dealings with each other as well as with clients and suppliers and other stakeholders. We would not consider a company that systematically lies to customers about availability or quality of its products or services as being honest or demonstrating integrity. Nor would we look favorably at a boss who promises a big raise to people and then changes her mind or finds reasons why the raises cannot be made. As noted, truthfulness is not the whole picture of integrity, but it is one major element. It is easy to see how honesty is important in business, and that to have a solidly-based organization you want to make sure that people in it demonstrate this kind of behavior.

The picture goes beyond simple honesty, however. To have a well-founded and sustainable organization you want to have people whose actions are morally solid as well. You don't want to see discrimination against women or minorities in most societies (with exceptions such as Taliban-led or ISIS-led societies). You don't want to see unfair treatment of people according to the whims of managers. So, in addition to truthfulness, you want to see a moral basis for actions that reflects what are considered today to be relevant human rights such as equal treatment of people.

The management consulting executive said that integrity is fairly simple in his view. The firm has a set of operating principles that represent who they are. He asserts that you can build integrity by celebrating great performance and abhorring failure to uphold the principles, such as always supporting your colleagues. He pointed to a very simple example of getting support, when he needed a phone charger in the evening while visiting a city away from home. He called the local office of the firm, and within an hour someone brought a charger to his hotel. Simple but powerful. And as a clear example of failure to uphold the principles: if someone were to criticize a colleague in front of a client – that would be grounds for termination. The rules are very clear, and the consultants know that the firm is standing behind them all the time. Integrity is acting in accord with these principles.

This is an interesting observation, since I will bet that not everyone wants to put such emphasis in their own firm on the specific kinds of integrity mentioned in this last example. Surely, we don't want people in the organization stabbing each other in the back to get ahead, but at the same time we may not view that failure to jump to support a colleague when in need is really that important. We may feel that our organization wants to emphasize integrity by putting fair treatment of women and minorities as a primary target for everyone, and that demonstration of this characteristic is the most important element of integrity. And I imagine that honesty in dealing with other people is probably a higher priority than any of these issues; the point is that integrity does matter in organizations, though it may be exemplified differently in different ones.

A very different view of integrity comes from the executive in construction equipment manufacturing. He says that the CEO demonstrates honesty in his dealings with everyone – and that if someone is caught lying in the company, that person is simply terminated. The executive pointed out that on a couple of occasions an employee was caught stealing from the company, and again these people immediately lost their jobs. The company treats people well, and it expects them to treat the company well, too.

He notes that: "Task completion is really important, and if you don't achieve that, you don't stay around. For example, launching a new product, or carrying out a project". You don't have to make every new product a success or have each project work out as hoped – but you do have to pursue the work with solid effort and commitment.

White lies about the business

What about the need for a company to paint a credible and positive picture to the employees as well as to external stakeholders, starting with the shareholders? This is a fascinating issue, that probably cannot be resolved in our discussion – but which is a major challenge nevertheless. During the last major crisis before Covid-19, the Global Financial Crisis, our bank was rife with rumors about expected layoffs due to the dramatic downturn in business that had occurred and that showed no sign of improving in early 2009. I vividly remember sitting with the Executive Committee, where the CEO said that we would not lay off anyone due to the crisis, and it was up to each of us division heads to get the word out to our employees through a meeting with all of them who could attend.

How could you make a credible statement to people whose jobs were on the line, when our banking business had dropped overall perhaps 10% below the level of the previous year? Other banks and companies were laying off people, and the mood was pretty grim. We decided to let the bank's earnings suffer a bit by telling our employees that no one would be laid off. This left us with lower revenues but not lower costs – expecting that the crisis would end in a reasonably short period of time. (The unstated managerial reality was that if the crisis lasted for more than a year or so, we probably would have to make layoffs, but that was far down the road.)

This was a real crisis situation in which it was important to keep up a good face to both the employees and the public that our organization was not going to fail, or even to have major problems. Of course, credibility is fundamental to banks, and we had to make sure that our creditworthiness did not drop dramatically. Luckily, we had no exposure to US mortgage loans or mortgage-backed bonds, so our hit from the financial crisis was due to reduced overall business activity rather than any losses on any particular investments or loans. I think that our performance in dealing with our people and our image was admirable; and when the crisis did end, we were seen as a reliable employer.

But what if your organization really was hurt severely by the crisis? If you were a bank or any other organization with investments or loans that incurred losses due to the crisis, you presumably would have tried to paint a picture of strength despite that situation. Otherwise, a run on the bank could bring down your business, as happened with Lehman Brothers, that did fail, and also with Countrywide Financial and Merrill Lynch that were forced to sell themselves to Bank of America, and with Bear Stearns and Washington Mutual that agreed to be acquired by JP Morgan. Just the appearance of weakness is enough to cause a run on the bank, as has happened through history, and so making positive statements despite (temporary) financial weakness is a necessary part of managing a financial institution.

How far should this kind of positioning go? If you want to increase your company's share price in the market, you could paint a rosier-than-realistic picture of your expected future sales and profits. And similarly, within the company you would want to keep employees comfortable with being there, even if some layoffs are in the wings. This is quite a slippery slope! I suppose that the only way to draw a line in behavior that shows integrity versus behavior that is harmfully misleading is to say that the white lies are justifiable if they support the well-being of the company and of society more broadly. After the fact we can see many differences between the statements of large US banks saying that they were solid, despite the financial crisis in the fall of 2008, versus the statements of Enron that its accounts were fairly presenting the company's business situation before that company spectacularly failed in 2001, or Elizabeth Holmes's misrepresentations of Theranos blood testing company, that failed in 2018. Or better yet, between the statements of companies that have temporary business shocks that managers believe will be overcome, versus Bernie Madoff creating the world's biggest Ponzi scheme and running it for decades before crashing in 2008.

White lies about people

How do you deal with the fact that some employees are more outgoing than others? Or that some employees are dedicated to grinding out work efforts, while others are much better at figuring out novel solutions to problems, and others are better at dealing with people? You don't want to try to force everyone into the same behavior or style, but you do want to get excellent performance out of everyone. I find this to be a tough challenge, in the sense that I find it useful sometimes to tell white lies about the performance of one employee to others, to try to build up that person's image in the eyes of colleagues. I will tell others that Rodney did a great job in solving a challenge in delivery of our services to a particular client – which was true, but I won't tell them that I harangued Rodney to get him going on the task until he did do it. Or I will say to others in our team that Daniela came up with an excellent way of reorganizing our client information so that it is much easier to work with now, even though I am aware that she is looking for a job elsewhere – but I want to keep her because of her good results.

Maybe these are not white lies at all. I am just failing to point out the weaknesses in a person's performance, while praising the strengths. Ideally, I would like for everyone to perform well and to encourage other members of the team. But just like with a bank's financial weakness in light of a financial crisis elsewhere, I don't want to rock the boat and give people an excuse for taking a negative view of someone on our team because of some weakness. You could perhaps say that this is integrity in the political science sense of trying to keep the organization whole, and functioning as a strong unit, rather than in a business sense of simply being honest. The point is that is that I don't feel that I am demonstrating less integrity by trying to get the best performance out of the team, even though I am shading my description of someone's performance in a rosy light.

Ethics in decision-making

Perhaps another way to look at the second part of integrity, namely following a moral compass, is to label it ethical behavior. The first part of integrity is honesty, and with the exception of the white lies discussed above, that idea is pretty clear. What should we use for a basis in defining ethical decision-making?

According to Brown and Treviño (2006, p. 595) ethical leadership is "the demonstration of normatively appropriate conduct through personal actions and interpersonal relationships, and the promotion of such conduct to followers through two-way communication, reinforcement, and decision-making". They found in an empirical study that 'ethical' leaders were ones "who were thought to be honest and trustworthy … [and] who were seen as fair and principled decision-makers who care about people and the broader society" (p.597). So, in their analysis, honesty was a key underpinning of ethical leadership, along with caring about people and holding to moral principles.

Note that we are interested in *ethical decision-making* by leaders, rather than the broader topic of ethical leadership. This may seem to be splitting hairs, but ethical leadership is conceptualized as not just decision-making, but it also includes demonstrating altruism, having a people orientation and even power sharing (e.g., Resick et al. 2006; Kalshoven et al. 2011). So, the dimensions of ethical leadership go beyond our focus, even though the other dimensions also can contribute to successful management of an organization.

Ron Carucci (2016) points out that organizational pressures may make it difficult for people to act ethically. For example, if a company sets unrealistically high targets for sales or profits, or unrealistically low targets for costs, this may drive managers to fudge the figures in order to meet those goals. It is very easy for an outside observer to say that the manager should not fake the data – but when you are in the organization and being pressured to produce good results, it is very difficult to resist the temptation of inflating those results. A logical direction for the pressured manager to go is to try to get a review of the targets and a reformulation based on realistic possible outcomes. This may be easier said than done; Carucci is right that organizational pressures really can create a moral hazard for managers.

Does honesty pay?

There is a real paradox in our discussion of integrity. If you look at business behavior in successful companies, you find that the leaders of many of them have lied or made misleading statements about their business over the years. The Harvard Business School (HBS) has been criticized in the past for training people who can do successful business without regard to moral behavior. This was vividly illustrated with Jeff Skilling, an HBS graduate who was CEO of Enron at the time of its massive fraud and collapse – and who was sentenced to 14 years in prison for his crimes there. There are quite a few other examples of HBS graduates who were caught in extremely unethical and often illegal behavior – but there are likely 50 or a 100 times as many HBS graduates who did not pursue such behavior, and many of whom have been very successful.

The point is not that there are bad apples in any barrel, which is surely true, but that unethical or illegal acts do not get punished very often in business, so it is difficult to say that honesty pays. An article in the *Harvard Business Review* many years ago (Bhide and Stevenson 1990) argued that, while honesty does not pay, it does give the honest person a moral basis for acting and a self-fulfilling reason for making decisions and building a life-style. According to those authors,

> The importance of moral and social motives in business cannot be overemphasized. A selective memory, a careful screening of the facts may help sustain the fiction of profitable virtue, but the fundamental basis of trust is moral. We keep promises because we believe it is right to do so, not because it is good business.
>
> (p.7)

Brown and Treviño (2006) found that ethical leadership is correlated with follower satisfaction, motivation and commitment to the organization. This contributes to ethical decision-making in the organization, since "the followers of ethical leaders should be more likely to focus on the ethical implications of their decisions and make more ethical decisions as a result" (p.607). And all of this supports a conclusion that ethical leadership is likely to lead to superior company performance, in any culture or country.

Similarly, Engelbrecht et al. (2017) found in South Africa that ethical leadership generated trust in the leader as well as greater engagement by employees with the organization. In other words, when a manager displayed ethical leadership in the workplace, this resulted in greater trust of employees in that manager, and consequently greater commitment of the employees to the organization. These authors did not look at the further question of whether or not the example set by the manager led to more ethical decision-making by the employees. These findings do support the argument that honesty (integrity) pays for the organization by generating a more motivating work environment.

The precise definition of integrity may differ to some extent between cultures (Mann et al. 2016). One consumer products executive said that in his experience at one of the largest consumer products companies, in Europe and in India, integrity really is viewed differently in different countries, because the terms of reference are not the same. In a European country, integrity has more to do with your responsibility to the company, while in India it also has to include your responsibilities to your family. Your decision-making and your commitments have to reflect both of these concerns or perspectives in the India subsidiary of the company.

On the other hand, this executive said that if you ask what behavior works to convey integrity in an organization, then the boss should demonstrate it by his/her actions, and subordinates will mimic the behavior of the boss. This was true in any country where the executive has worked. This is an interesting challenge, however. If an executive is transferred to an Indian subsidiary of the company, he/she needs to learn what behavior demonstrates integrity in that context, viz., commitment to both your family and your company. When later transferred to a European country, the executive has to take stock of the meaning of integrity in that culture, and try to behave accordingly. Cultural differences in this context do matter!

What about corruption?

Perhaps the most visible or at least the most widely discussed issue when talking about integrity of people in business is corruption. Corruption involves dishonest or fraudulent conduct by someone in a position of power, often in government, when dealing with business. This is common in the case of bribery, where a government official takes some financial or other benefit from a company in exchange for favorable treatment, such as awarding a contract, offering a favorable regulatory treatment or ignoring legal restrictions on a business activity. It is clearly a biased way to treat the company, and it involves unethical behavior from both the government official and the company manager/executive (e.g., D'Souza et al. 2013).

There are many spectacular examples of corporate bribery of government officials: Kellogg Brown & Root paid millions of dollars to officials in the government of Nigeria to win a natural gas plant construction contract in 2008 and was fined about $600 million in the United States; Siemens paid bribes of over $1 billion to government officials in Asia, Europe, Africa and Latin America over more than ten years to win electrical equipment sales contracts which were uncovered in 2006, and paid fines of over $1 billion to the governments of the United States and Germany; the Brazilian construction company, Odebrecht, paid bribes of more than $4 billion to government officials in a dozen countries, mostly in Latin America, and in Operation Lava Jato was brought to task and fined about $1 billion by the Brazilian government in 2014; the Gupta family in South Africa bribed President Zuma and numerous other government officials to win hundreds of millions of dollars of contracts with Eskom (electric power), Transnet (transportation company) and other government entities, finally discovered in 2017. Airbus in 2020 agreed to pay $4 billion in fines to the governments of France, the United Kingdom and the United States for bribery of foreign officials in 16 countries over the course of the previous decade. (See, for example, www.transparency.org/en/news/25-corruption-scandals and www.investopedia.com/financial-edge/0512/the-biggest-bribe-cases-in-business-history.aspx.) These are very large bribery scandals, and they just touch the surface of the problem around the world.

Laws such as the US Foreign Corrupt Practices Act of 1977 made such bribery illegal for companies operating in the United States, and this initial foray has led to similar laws being passed in dozens of other countries in subsequent years (www.globalcompliancenews.com/anti-corruption/anti-corruption-laws-around-the-world/). Today the rules are much tighter around the issue of company attempts to bribe government officials, but there is no doubt that the problem persists. It seems that dishonesty of this kind does indeed pay, even with the threat of legal sanctions in place. That is, the risk of getting caught, along with the penalties that have been applied in such cases, are much smaller than the gains from the corrupt behavior (e.g., D'Souza and Kaufmann 2013; Gauthier et al. 2021). In contrast, Kaufmann and Wei (2000) found that firms that pay more bribes end up spending more managerial time dealing with bureaucrats than firms that don't, and the bribing firms also had a higher cost of capital – so the simple conclusion that the risk of getting caught is low hides the fact that engaging in bribery is a costly activity to the firm.

Do people from different cultures see corruption differently?

There are many examples of high levels of corruption in countries such as Venezuela, Syria, Equatorial Guinea and Somalia (as measured by Transparency International, www.transparency.org/en/cpi/2020/index/nzl). The press talks about 'kleptocracies' and 'lawless states' in reference to these countries, and no doubt the level of corruption is higher there than in, say, Denmark or Sweden. But do people in such countries, and in different countries around the world, really see corruption differently?

I think that it just depends on the terms of reference. If we go back to the example of driving above the speed limit, it is just a widely socially accepted practice in probably most or all countries. If we talk about bribing government officials on the scale of the Odebrecht scandal in Brazil or the Jacob Zuma–related scandals in South Africa, then this is a phenomenon that is much less common and much more condemned across countries. Even so, it is a question of degree, rather than saying that some countries are corrupt or that some are populated by wanton lawbreakers, and other countries are not.

From experience in Venezuela and in South Africa, I have seen many more routine examples of bribing government officials to get favorable treatment than in the United States. And from living in Luxembourg and also working in Switzerland, I have seen and read about much less bribery being uncovered in those countries. Based on these experiences, I would say that this particular kind of unethical behavior is indeed more common in some countries than others. But again, it is not as if any country is immune to the problem of bribery and corruption.

Think for a moment, however, about the time and effort that must be spent in many countries to get legal permissions to do business or even to get a driver's license. The cost of bureaucracy is extreme in some cases, and I think that most of us would cut corners to get things done, just as we do with exceeding speed limits. In India, the famous 'license raj' was (and still is in many instances) a government bureaucrat who had to give permission for various business activities, from getting a driver's license to setting up a legal business to obtaining permissions for many activities (Majumdar 2004). And businesses would routinely pay off the license raj to obtain the permission needed, or to obtain it much faster. This may not be corruption on the scale of Odebrecht or the Guptas, but it is certainly the same kind of rule-bending. A prescriptive conclusion in these less-egregious situations would be to push for designing a more sensible set of rules rather than to fight against corruption alone.

Conclusions

How important are honesty and integrity in business? They are helpful for demonstrating a leadership style that motivates employees, and so they are desirable kinds of behavior. They are certainly not sufficient to guarantee a company's success, but they are valuable traits of leaders that encourage followers. Across cultures and countries, honesty and integrity produce similar benefits in organizations, although the exceptions of behavior such as bribery are quite striking and fairly different across countries (Koehn 2005).

In today's world where Democrats and Republicans in the United States seem to see different facts about the same event and about people despite physical evidence, it is easy to understand how differences in views of honesty and integrity can exist. This makes it very difficult for companies and other organizations to promote a culture of integrity. Even so, as shown throughout this chapter, people generally like to work in organizations where leaders are honorable and who demonstrate integrity.

Corruption is a particularly pernicious form of the lack of integrity in business. Corruption exists around the world, and perhaps we can argue that it is more prevalent in countries that have more rules for running a business. Corruption requires a business person and a government official to participate, such that the government person receives a benefit from bending or breaking the rules, and the business person obtains benefits such as a license to operate or some kind of government protection from competitors. With government efforts such as the Foreign Corrupt Practices Act in the United States, and similar policies in other countries in recent years, the effort to reduce corruption has become widespread. Just like the pursuit of Sustainable Development Goals (the UN targets), the goal of reducing corruption is making progress.

So, while honesty and integrity certainly do not characterize all companies in all countries, there does seem to be a global trend toward bolstering such behavior. The pressure from Millennials and Gen Z people who are coming to dominate the workforce will continue to push this agenda for the foreseeable future.

References

Becker, Thomas, 1998. Integrity in organizations: Beyond honesty and conscientiousness. *The Academy of Management Review*, 23(1) January, 154–61.

Bhide, Amar, and Howard Stevenson, 1990. Why be honest if honesty doesn't pay?. *Harvard Business Review*. September–October. 1–9.

Brown, Michael and Linda K. Treviño, 2006. Ethical leadership: A review and future directions. *The Leadership Quarterly*, 17, 595–616.

Carucci, Ron, 2016. Why ethical people make unethical choices. *Harvard Business Review*. Digital edition. https://hbr.org/2016/12/why-ethical-people-make-unethical-choices

D'Souza, Anna, and Daniel Kaufmann, 2013. Who bribes in public contracting and why: Worldwide evidence from firms. *Economics of Governance*, 14, 333–67.

Engelbrecht, Amos, Gardielle Heine, and Bright Mahembe, 2017. Integrity, ethical leadership, trust and work engagement. *Leadership & Organization Development Journal*, 38(3), 368–79.

Gauthier, Bernard, Jonathan Goyette, and Wilfried A.K. Kouamé, 2021. Why do firms pay bribes? Evidence on the demand and supply sides of corruption in developing countries. *Journal of Economic Behavior and Organization*, 190, 463–79.

Kalshoven, K., Deanne N. Den Hartog, and Annebel H.B. De Hoogh, 2011. Ethical leadership at work questionnaire (ELW): development and validation of a multi-dimensional measure", *The Leadership Quarterly*, 22(1), 51–69.

Kaufmann, Daniel, and Shang-Jin Wei, 2000. "Does 'grease money' speed up the wheels of commerce?". *IMF Working Paper No. 00/64*. www.imf.org/en/Publications/WP/Issues/2016/12/30/Does-Grease-Money-Speed-Up-the-Wheels-of-Commerce-3524

Koehn, Daryl, 2005. Integrity as a Business Asset. *Journal of Business Ethics*, 58, 125–36.

Majumdar, Sumit, 2004. The hidden hand and the license raj: An evaluation of the relationship between age and the growth of firms in India. *Journal of Business Venturing*, 19, 107–25.

Mann, Heather, Ximena Garcia-Rada, Lars Hornuf, Juan Tafurt, and Dan Ariely, 2016. Cut from the same cloth: Similarly dishonest individuals across countries. *Journal of Cross-Cultural Psychology*, 47(6), 858–74.

Resick, C.J., Paul J. Hanges, Marcus W. Dickson, and Jacqueline K. Mitchelson, 2006. A cross-cultural examination of the endorsement of ethical leadership. *Journal of Business Ethics*, 63(4), 345–59.

Chapter 8

Planning, looking forward

Introduction

The treatment of time is one element of human behavior that cross-cultural analysts like to emphasize because of clear differences in how time is viewed, what 'on-time' means, and how long of a perspective people take in different cultures. For North Americans time tends to be very linear, goals and deadlines have serious time dimensions, and a forward-looking element is important. For Latin Americans, generalizing perhaps too much, time is less strictly viewed: meetings scheduled for 10 am may actually start at 10:15 or 10:30, and everyone accepts that this is normal and appropriate. Likewise, due to more economic and sometimes political volatility in Latin America, people tend to look at short periods of time, in months for example, when planning business activities. For longer periods there are too many unknown factors that will affect business, so companies tend to plan less precisely than in the United States. Asians in many cases view time as somewhat circular rather than linear, so for example animals are born, live and die and then return to live again. In the organizational context this implies that some activities are circular and repeated, such as coming to work and going home, and eating and sleeping, which are repeated every day. There are other aspects of work that are more linear, such as building a product or providing a service. Even in this context, the picture can be viewed as circular, since once a transportation or financial service has been provided one time, it likely will be provided similarly again in the future.

These ideas all go to say that time is not viewed similarly by everyone or in all contexts. Even so, there is one aspect of time that is very important in business, namely the time that a business is operating profitably. If a company does not produce profits, then eventually it will have to be shut down, maybe excepting charities and NGOs (and of course governments and some government-owned companies) that are not expected to produce profits. Ignoring these exceptions, if a business cannot produce its product or service profitably, then it will cease to exist at some point. So, the future is important

DOI: 10.4324/9781003367512-8

in business, since a company must consider how to compete successfully today and in the future if it wants to remain in operation.

A key question is: How far forward should the company be thinking and planning? Thinking and planning for a few months is necessary, just to make sure that the company prepares to buy inputs and find customers for future production and sales. But what about planning for the next five or ten years? If technology changes, if regulation changes or if new competitors enter the company's market, then what should be done? These questions should be considered on a regular basis, looking forward for at least several years, so that the company will not be overwhelmed by some change in conditions that is unexpected, without having at least a sketch of a strategic response ready for such eventualities.

One can readily imagine that, in an emerging market such as Bolivia or Kenya or Thailand, companies need to be prepared for unexpected occurrences, for example major changes in government policies – at the same time as they should be thinking about the potential entry of companies from the Triad (the United States, the EU, and Japan) or companies from other emerging markets. Even in the United States companies have to be concerned with changes in technology in such areas as telecommunication, transportation and computing that may affect their business in the future due to entry by new companies or reorganized supply chains.

So, how far should we look into the future? Before tackling this question let's back up and think about how forward-looking we want our organizations to be. If our company is a bank or other financial service provider, how should we think about the future? We probably don't want our tellers and our operations people worrying too much about large changes in the business, except as those changes may affect their jobs – such as implementation of a new enterprise resource planning (ERP) system like SAP or Oracle or Acumatica or Sage Intacct. If the organization adopts one of these ERP systems, that likely means a steep learning curve for many people, including frontline customer-facing people as well as back-office staff in operations.

But we also don't want just top management to worry about the future, when awareness of new challenges may come from people at any level of the organization, and you want to get that information to decision-makers quickly. This chapter looks in a structured way at some of the key issues involved in dealing with the future.

Is forward-looking behavior important to your organization?

In any organization it is valuable to have people thinking about the future. If employees just do their jobs without regard to improving the way they work and/or the efficiency of that work, then the company will fail to advance when it could. This is likely to leave the company behind competitors who do have employees looking for ways to improve their work.

It is a longer stretch to say that people in the organization should be thinking about the future and what might come up as opportunities or threats to the company's business. An office staff person does not need to envision future business and how it may change from current circumstances. But at the same time, you would like staff people to pay some attention to how the competitor down the street (say a store or a restaurant) is operating, and how your organization is more or less efficient or customer-friendly or otherwise better/worse than the rival. So, for one thing, we could say that the organization wants everybody to be looking out for opportunities to do the business more efficiently and to generate more purchases from customers. And you would also like a smaller number of people looking at the company's competitive position, possible upcoming changes in regulation or competitors and changes in technology that may affect the business.

In this way there are perhaps two kinds of forward-looking behavior that may be helpful to the company. The first is the idea of encouraging people to observe how their work is being done, and for them to look for opportunities to improve on the activities and processes that they are following. People at any level of the organization can do this, and it is probably done in at least an informal manner everywhere. This idea was enshrined in business literature when the Japanese system of 'kaizen' was identified by Imai (1986) in the 1980s. Kaizen means 'continuous improvement', and it can be pursued by anyone at any level of the organization.

This idea of kaizen originated in Japan, though the focus on paying attention to details in the production process appears to have originated in the United States, perhaps with Walter Shewhart at Bell Laboratories in the 1920s. Shewhart worked primarily in statistical control processes, but his intent was to improve the quality of production processes, often through small changes in such processes to eliminate defects or mistakes. He developed the Plan-Do-Check-Act continuous improvement cycle, or Shewhart Cycle, of analyzing a production process to find errors and then to correct them (Shewhart 1931).

The overall kaizen concept is described by Mcpherson et al. (2015, p. 40):

> Kaizen is the result of management's engagement of the organization to pursue business excellence through the interplay between management's pursuit of profit and competition, and employees' skills, creativity, confidence and pride. Management and employees are then codependent through the development and acquisition of multiple tools and methods – the observable outputs we see – that create an energy across and through the organization that in turn encourages employees to seek and achieve proactive change and innovation.

Thus, forward-looking behavior is central to kaizen thinking, and both workers and managers contribute to it.

The second type of forward-looking behavior is the structured, planning activity that many or most organizations go through either annually or more frequently. This activity is usually set up as a process through which leaders within the organization meet on this infrequent basis to specific- ally address challenges and opportunities that are anticipated for the year (or semester) ahead. Usually a discussion among members of the leadership team is used to try to identify key issues to be looked at in more detail and for recommendations that can then be presented to top management. Also, longer-term issues (perhaps 2–5 years out) are intended to be included in the discussion, although frequently such issues are mentioned but not ser- iously considered in preparing the company to deal with the future.

This strategic planning process is both important to get the company's leaders to think constructively about fairly near-term challenges and oppor- tunities – as well as a source of endless jokes about the attention paid to elaborating a plan that never sees the light of day once it has been written. So, hopefully it is obvious: the importance is in the process of thinking about the issues rather than on the concrete written result of the exercise. Strategic planning is explored in more detail below.

How do people demonstrate forward-looking behavior in an organization?

If I think of my bank, the only forward-looking behavior that was regularly produced was the economic forecast by our chief economist on staff (other than kaizen-like efforts by individual people to improve their work results). He gave weekly updates including forecasts of macroeconomic measures such as inflation, interest rates and growth of the national economy. He also looked slightly less frequently at the exchange rate, unemployment and at other topical subjects such as trade with China or the expected impact in South Africa (home of our headquarters) of events in the EU.

In addition to our economist's forecasts, we only received anecdotal com- mentaries from members of the executive committee about major issues that looked likely to affect us, such as a potential change in government policy toward the banking sector, an anticipated union strike or protest or changes in market share of our bank versus the three main rivals in the country. While we said that considering challenges that were coming along in the future was important to our organization, we did not do anything specific (outside of the annual strategic planning process). I should add that our CEO attended a wide variety of banking sector meetings, international meetings of various types, conferences on topics where he spoke and other assorted activities that kept him regularly in touch with what other firms were doing, and with what the government and other stakeholders cared about. Through his activities the bank was provided with input about issues that we should pay attention to in the future.

One major way that most organizations look forward is to project expected sales of their services or products in the fairly near-term future, say for a year or two. This is a necessary condition for managing inventories, supply chain purchases and a myriad of other details of running a business. This may not seem especially futuristic, but it is certainly an important element of operating a successful business, and it is true in any country or culture. And it is relevant at all levels of the organization, from maintenance people keeping track of their stocks of cleaning supplies to cell phone assemblers paying attention to the availability of chips and other components, to corporate leaders trying to find better ways to compete with rivals and increase future sales.

A small business owner told me that

> Forward-looking behavior is demonstrated when people are able and willing to innovate by doing things that are necessary to achieve the organization's goals instead of just doing things "in their usual way". The need for it and how it is demonstrated is similar in the US and Latin America, but it is more prevalent in the US because of cultural factors like more flexible organizational hierarchy and labor laws, and greater appreciation for individualism and innovation.

This is very interesting, because it notes both that kaizen-type behavior is common, and that it is more likely to be carried out in the United States rather than in Latin America, where hierarchies are more rigid.

A corporate executive in supply chain management told me that:

> It's about creating a culture that continuously challenges the norms. It is about encouraging people to try new things, without fear of failure (within reason, of course). I try and encourage this all the time – try new things – fantastic if it works and pays off – if it does not we have learnt what not to do. It does work – as people within my business are always finding ways to do things better – technology as an enabler is constantly evolving, we lead when it comes to FM technology especially in the engineering sector. Innovation is also driven as part of our KPI process and linked to bonuses and remuneration. This does encourage people to think differently.

Another corporate executive in a Middle Eastern manufacturing conglomerate said that:

> Being forward looking is a skill one learns and a process that is built into the company. I describe a person who is forward-looking to be able to

"see around corners." Everyone can plan out three months and make budget decisions against day-to-day operations; every company can have a grandiose five-year plan (who knows what will happen in five years; you can almost say anything!). But being able to make decisions and spend capital that will affect the company in 6–18 months from now is probably the hardest decision to make. This is the timeframe when bigger bets need to be made and bigger bets have a longer pay-back or return period.

Seeing around corners requires an executive to be able to hold multiple theories for the future simultaneously. Too often, an executive will become wedded to a particular idea or notion; they become very emotional, end up spending too much time or money on the idea, and it ends up being a loser. Seeing around corners requires an executive to hold all those ideas in their mind, gather new infor-mation on all of them, entertain conversations with insiders and outsiders, and over a period of time, whittle the options down. In this process, new learnings and information will cause the options origin-ally considered to mature, change, merge, or drop. By being patient in being forward looking, a good executive will save significant time, energy, and money.

Patience can go against conventional wisdom in a go-go world; but great ideas need time to incubate. The criteria and urgency around operational execution should not be automatically assumed for incu-bating an idea to drive the strategy of the firm.

How can a leader increase the forward-looking behavior of employees?

Since thinking about the future is a valuable attribute for an organization's people, how can a leader stimulate constructive behavior that produces such thinking? In a long-existing company, the process of thinking about the future is probably well-established in strategic planning and in mechanisms to encourage line workers to seek kaizen improvements on a continuous basis. In a newer company, these processes need to be established and ingrained into the work force.

A simple way to encourage forward-looking behavior is to embody that goal in performance indicators (KPI's) used in people's job assignments, as noted above in the supply chain management business. In any company, if a staff or clerical person is offered a bonus for coming up with an idea that will save time or money, this kind of behavior can be stimulated. If a manager or executive participates in the annual strategic planning process, then he/she will be encouraged to think about future challenges and opportunities that the organization may face. Especially if people can get the feeling that when they come up with a great idea to do something new or different, they will likely receive the opportunity to pursue that idea, it can be greatly stimulating.

According to the executive in construction equipment manufacturing,

> [our employees] know they will be evaluated, and they want a raise, so they had better be forward looking to help the company do better and thus help themselves do better. We don't have to justify our profits every quarter, since we are a private company. In our Friday meetings we decide what we need in order to succeed, and then spend what is needed to get there.

These Friday meetings push the managers and executives to focus on the upcoming needs and opportunities of the company on a regular, frequent basis.

Another way to encourage forward-looking behavior is through the corporate vision and mission statements. According to the supply chain management executive,

> In my view, it is extremely important to have a very clearly defined but simple Vision for the company that everyone can identify with. It should be widely communicated and get everyone to "live" the vision and values of the company. Strong and regular communication sessions must be held diligently, where progress is articulated, shortcomings are identified and remedial plans put into place. Buy-in is critical from all levels. Just as important is celebrating the wins, and building upon them. Knowing and identifying what needs to be achieved in the future, keeps people set on striving for the "prize".

In my bank in Africa, senior executives were strongly encouraged to look at what other financial service providers and other relevant competitors were doing, and to seek out directions for us to go to match or beat those strategies. We discussed these issues almost every week at our weekly executive team meeting, and there was strong buy-in from all of us to offer examples of what competitors were doing and how we could respond. For example, we looked frequently at what other banks were doing to serve lower- and middle-income clients, since they make up the vast majority of South Africans, and the government was pressuring us to do more to serve them. Because it is difficult to find profitable ways to serve those segments of the market, we tried many different initiatives and tried to find good ideas from our local competitors and others throughout Africa where we had operations.

We also talked about what our bank could do to fend off competition from foreign entrants into our market, and how we could build up business with China through the equity link that we sold to ICBC there. These initiatives all came from looking at our ongoing business, and thinking about adjustments to make that could enhance our competitive position. We did very little "blue sky" thinking, about possible new business opportunities or countries to consider for doing business and so forth. That is, we looked forward to some extent, but our thinking was very limited to managing and extending the ongoing business. We invited an executive program director from abroad to talk with our executive team one weekend, and he elicited from all of us that we spent at least 80% of our time dealing with day-to-day issues of the organization, and at most 20% considering somewhat new directions, almost all of which were adjustments to our existing activities. I will bet that this is not uncommon for other organizations – not just banks – as well.

According to the executive in the manufacturing conglomerate,

> We built into our company what we called a "strategy and budgeting process." This involved setting a strategy for the firm, allocating a budget, and then getting the budget approved by the Board. By making this into a process, instead of discrete events, we all became adept at making strategy a continual conversation. We were constantly discussing strategy as we made hiring decisions, HR policy, budget allocations for surprise business opportunities, and marketing documentation. When strategy becomes a process instead of an event, people start to become forward looking and make decisions based on not just today, but also their belief in the future. This is important as they will be reviewed and rated against the soundness of the decisions they made. In doing so, taking into account what is happening now and what we want to make happen in the future is important. Creating this strategy and budgeting process was one of the keys to our success in operational excellence and beating the competition.

Is planning ahead important for people in your organization? How? Why?

In a simple sense, planning ahead is a critical function of managers: "Scanning the environment and assessing uncertainty are among the most important managerial activities in strategizing and decision-making" (Tapinos and Pyper 2018, p.292). Those authors go on to explore how companies produce forward-looking analysis, principally by using scenario planning and other strategic planning tools. And they emphasize the importance of collaborative thinking, that is, sharing among decision-makers the measures and models about the future that a company may use, to draw understanding of possible future conditions and then to create steps for the organization to take to deal with that future.

The idea of collaboration may be the most important element of forward thinking in an organization. If leaders of the organization talk together about where the organization is going and what challenges may occur to pursuing that objective, it is more likely that the organization will develop a reasoned approach to dealing with the challenges and achieving the goals. This goes for workers/staff as well, in the sense that kaizen improvements will be shared more effectively if people talk with colleagues about what those improvements are. And of course we need to recognize that anyone in the organization may come up with a brilliant idea for greater success, so the collaboration with others is key.

How can you foster that collaboration? It is not difficult to point to mechanisms such as weekly meetings of managers of a division or meetings of staff in any area, which will encourage sharing of ideas and observations of how the company is doing. I know that in my division of the bank the weekly meetings, which typically occupied an hour on Tuesday mornings, provided very valuable guidance on improving our performance – and motivation for the managers to make suggestions as well.

When asked if it is important for his organization's people in managerial/ executive positions, the supply chain management executive said:

> There should always be a balance between doing things right in the present, but also looking ahead to maintain results and strive for excellence and growth. The future of the company should always be important, as one of the key success factors for any company should be long term sustainability. Also looking at the future will to a large extent mitigate complacency, especially if a company is successful in the present. Longer term scanning, risk and opportunity identification should be built into the organisation, especially in times of ever-increasing competition and the evolution of technology at such a phenomenal pace. The Top Management of the company have to continuously look at reinventing itself to be better and more efficient. Stagnation spells disaster, as the competition will start to eat away at your market share. Innovation should be a culture within any organisation.

Is forward-looking behavior stymied by uncontrollable conditions?

A number of people have told me over the years that it is extremely difficult to plan ahead in an environment where government policies change sometimes capriciously, when a different government takes power or when economic conditions deteriorate severely. So, forward-looking behavior is discouraged due to the lack of ability to anticipate the policy changes or severe economic downturns. It seems to me a little excessive to view the future as being so uncontrollable, because a company can always make plans and then change them in response to a specific environmental change such as a new law or a political conflict or a pandemic(!). But it is true that when the environment is less predictable or at least less stable, it is harder to make plans and commitments that could be undone by unforeseen events such as regulation changes or civil unrest that affects the company's activities.[1] This is particularly problematic when the company has large fixed assets such as factories or mines, which are not easily shut down temporarily or moved to another location, as a services company might be able to do.

Even so, it is probably reasonable to assert that conditions in many emerging markets are less stable in the macroeconomic sense, and in terms of government policies, as well as in terms of other external-to-the-company factors such as weather, union activities, terrorism and others. When these conditions do affect company activities on a frequent basis or in a severe manner, then it is fair to say that strategic planning is very difficult to carry out. What may be more useful is to identify the key risks like these, and to plan steps for the company to take if the anticipated event takes place. Then planning may be done on a less-specific basis of setting targets for the period (year) ahead, and just establishing baselines goals while leaving greater details until the situation (e.g., labor protests, floods, prospective government policy changes toward business) has sorted itself out.

What about the situation for companies operating in Ukraine in 2022? Once Russia invaded the country in February, foreign and domestic companies alike faced an almost completely unpredictable war environment. No matter what your strategic planning might have envisioned last year, there is only a remote likelihood that you might have planned for a Russian invasion. Assuming that you indeed did not have any planning done for this event, then the actions of your company after the invasion started on February 24 would likely be to minimize war damage and possibly to shut down for some time to see how things develop. This is certainly a context in which strategic planning or kaizen efforts did not help, since no one anticipated the war. But once the war was underway, a company could plan for the next year with many contingencies depending on how the fighting and the negotiating go.

A similar phenomenon in unpredictability was the Covid-19 pandemic. How could a company have planned for that phenomenon, or even foreseen it? The answer is that you could not have done so, and the only managerial response was to react once the pandemic started. Thinking back to that time in March of 2020, no one knew how severe the infection would be, how long it might last and what to do to protect yourself. So, a forward-looking behavior really was just to react to the start of the pandemic with steps that seemed sensible, but with extreme uncertainty remaining. If you ran a restaurant, hotel, airline or even a store, your choices of strategy were severely limited by lockdowns and other antivirus measures that were implemented by governments around the world. It probably took at least three months to have a reasonable idea of what the coming year held for your business, and so you could have done some planning. But even there the impact was very different in different industries and in different countries. So, the only kind of conclusion that one might make is to respond to the health hazard of the pandemic and then make plans and revised plans on a frequent basis as the virus spread and mutated.

Can you measure forward-looking behavior?

If you want to generate forward-looking behavior in an organization, of course you need to be able to measure it somehow. The measure may be purely subjective, based on a boss' judgment of the performance of his/her direct reports. Or it may be based on some scale of observed behavior, for example, if the person has made any suggestion(s) for improving the way the business operates, or if the person has taken on some task that involved looking forward to business conditions or the company's activities in the future or if the person has contributed importantly to the annual strategic planning process. There are many possibilities for measuring, once your company decides that this behavior is important enough to measure and evaluate.

An interesting measure suggested by Preis et al. (2012) relates to a *country*'s forward-looking behavior. Their measure is the number of times that internet users in a country do Google searches for anything related to the coming year. This is compared with the number of times that internet users in that country do Google searches for anything related to the past year. In 2010 these authors looked at the number of times users in a country asked about 2011 in their searches, relative to the number of times they asked about 2009. They were able to obtain data on 45 countries, and they found that Germany, Switzerland and Japan led the list for the greatest forward-looking behavior. (The United States ranked 11th, and China ranked 41st.)

Within a company, although this would likely be questioned as intrusive activity with respect to employee privacy, if the IT department were to search internal emails to see who talks most about the year ahead versus the year behind. Or who talks about new projects or about subjects that are raised by management as major concerns or opportunities for the company to deal with in the future. If the specific forward-looking items can be chosen, then employee communications can be searched for those items, and scored for frequency or amount of discussion or some other measure. Even as I write this, I worry about the privacy of employees if this kind of measurement were done – so it is probably better if the company uses boss' opinions of their direct reports' forward-looking behavior.

How far forward should you look?

Publicly traded companies are often criticized for focusing only on the short term, since they need to report quarterly earnings to regulators and to the market. So, obviously decision-makers will try to show the best results possible on a quarterly basis. Any attempt to sacrifice short-term profits for long-term gains is a very difficult sell in the stock market. At the other extreme, John Maynard Keynes said that if we aim for returns in the long run, that is too far away to matter to current investors. In his words: "in the long run, we are all dead" (Keynes 1923). Is there a happy medium?

This is a bit of a red herring example, since a company can easily look to take measures that will help short-term earnings while at the same time planning for longer term such as 3–5 years in the future. If your company is an airline, then you need to obtain aircraft to transport your passengers. Buying an airplane creates a long-term commitment, since recuperating the approximately $100 million cost of one Airbus 320 or Boeing 737 will take a long time. Even so, the airline could potentially lease the aircraft instead of buying it, and that way avoid the huge fixed cost of ownership. This is somewhat like the choice between renting an apartment versus buying a house; the first is cheaper, but you build up no equity, and the latter is more expensive in terms of the fixed cost, but it allows you to benefit from rising home prices. Used airplanes generally do not go up in value, but they last for many years and they do have a final salvage value, so the decision to purchase is not necessarily a bad one.

The point here is that it is not necessary to choose between short-term and long-term considerations in decision-making. Both are important and they generally only conflict in the make-versus-buy (purchase-versus-rent) decision.

Conclusions

Any business needs to be forward-looking to some extent. In some cases such as general manufacturing and service provision, this largely just requires some amount of planning to ensure that supply chains are adequate to deal with ups and downs in demand and that costs are managed carefully. In other cases, such as producing fashionable clothes or internet platforms, there is enormous uncertainty about future demand and decisions may take on bet-the-company characteristics fairly often. Many businesses are in between these two extremes, but in all cases it is important to think carefully about the future and to strategize based on that thinking.

The length of time involved in forward planning may be longer in more stable economic environments, but even so the future is uncertain, and commitments of physical equipment, facilities and large amounts of money have to be made with caution. Emerging markets generally tend to be more volatile in terms of macroeconomic conditions as well as regulatory stability and also conditions in the business environment such as social unrest and political strife, so it certainly is more complicated to do planning in that context. Nevertheless, the main benefit of planning in the first place is to force decision-makers to think about future challenges and opportunities – and this is relevant in any country or industry context.

Note

1 This challenge was brought home to me by the service delivery protests in South Africa, which can bring a company's business to a halt. These protests involve protesters against lack of government-provided services such as electricity or water, or housing or education, who set up their protests in front of your business, or even damage your business with violent actions. This may be because your business is located next to a government office or a government project that is the actual target of the protest, and your company just faces 'collateral damage'. See Wocke and Grosse (2022).

References

Imai, Masaaki, 1986. *Kaizen: The Key to Japan's Competitive Success*. New York: McGraw-Hill/Irwin.

Keynes, John Maynard, 1923. *A Tract on Monetary Reform*. New York: Macmillan.

Macpherson, Wayne; Lockhart, James; Kavan, Heather; Iaquinto, Anthony, 2015. Kaizen: a Japanese philosophy and system for business excellence. *Journal of Business Strategy*, 36(5), 3–9.

Preis, Tobias, Helen Susannah Moat, H. Eugene Stanley, and Steven R. Bishop, 2012. Quantifying the advantage of looking forward. *Scientific Reports*, 2, 350.

Shewhart, Walter, A., 1931. *Economic Control of Quality of Manufactured Product*. New York: Van Nostrand.

Tapinos, Efstathios, and Neil Pyper, 2018. Forward looking analysis: Investigating how individuals 'do' foresight and make sense of the future. *Technological Forecasting and Social Change*, 126, 292–302.

Wocke, Albert, and Robert Grosse, 2022. Social protest action, stakeholder management and risk for small businesses: Managing the impact of service delivery protests in South Africa. (forthcoming).

Chapter 9

Why do people work?

Introduction

I originally considered this chapter as a discussion of how important income is to people, aiming to see if lower-income people would attach more importance to earning enough to make ends meet, and if higher-income people had a different perspective. But as I got into the chapter, I realized that a more useful question is: Why do people work? Is it just for income, or for satisfaction of having a place where your effort is valued, or for other reasons that might be identified? So, the chapter begins with a discussion of the fundamental goal of working to earn enough money to meet family needs, and then considers how needs are different in different contexts and then how other goals also drive people to work.

The concern about making ends meet is easy to understand in the context of the United States, where people with poverty-level incomes of less than $28,000 per year for a family of four in 2022 are considered poor. If your family income is, say, $75,000 per year, or about three times the poverty level, then you are not likely to worry nearly as much about making ends meet as the poor person – unless of course you have gone heavily into debt (e.g., for student loans) or face some other large financial burden (e.g., for healthcare). If your family income is in the $20,000 range, then for sure it is difficult to make ends meet.

What about in other countries? Probably in Germany or Switzerland, the income levels and concerns would be similar to those in the United States. In Mexico, or in South Africa, incomes are much lower, and people with annual family income of $28,000 would be considered middle class. These people in the emerging markets would likely not worry about making ends meet, whereas people earning $5 per day or less in Mexico, and those living on $2 per day or less in South Africa would definitely be considered poor and would have to worry about earning enough to pay for food, clothing and housing. There is no doubt that different countries display different levels of income that signify poverty – but poverty exists in all countries, and people at the lower end of the income scale have greater need of income to satisfy basic needs.

DOI: 10.4324/9781003367512-9

Once basic needs are covered, what else factors into people's thinking about work? Some kinds of jobs put a mind-numbing burden on people, such as working on an assembly line in manufacturing, or working on the food production line at a restaurant or in the back office of a bank or working in an Amazon fulfillment center. You might say that you would like to work more hours in one of these jobs, but it would probably be just to earn more income for purposes beyond basic needs. Of course, there is no doubt that some people prefer these kinds of jobs, and some specific jobs in this category are actually very attractive, so people might want to work more hours for more satisfaction and not just for more money.

For other kinds of jobs, it is more likely that people will want to work more hours because they enjoy the work and/or it is fulfilling in some sense. People who work in creative activities such as R&D or athletic or musical performance may wish to work more, because of the satisfaction of putting a new idea into practice, or the appreciation shown by an audience, or for the joy of winning a competition. Not the least of the considerations is satisfaction that other people view your work as valuable, and so self-satisfaction from feeling wanted in this way is quite understandable.

How important is meeting basic needs?

To someone sitting comfortably in her living room in the United States today, it may seem hard to believe that people do have trouble meeting basic needs. According to a Gallup poll just before the pandemic (Gallup 2020), it was found that only 1% of Americans stated this concern, which is probably not overwhelming, though it does mean over 3 million people felt that they could not ensure meeting their basic needs. If we switch to an emerging market such as Afghanistan or Benin, the percentage of people worried that they might not be able to meet basic needs was approximately half of the total population in 2019.

This picture of basic needs demonstrates, among other things, that the concerns of most people working in the United States or other Triad countries today are for things other than those basic needs. The other things could be Maslow-type higher-order needs (see Figure 9.1), such as feeling loved by family, or having self-esteem in the workplace, or feeling able to reach your potential. Or it could be as simple as keeping up with the Joneses, that is, having a lifestyle and material goods similar to your neighbors.

In an emerging market, Peru, one executive in a large non-profit organization said that "It is very important nowadays to have your employees satisfied so that they will concentrate on their jobs and not be thinking about getting a new one or a part time job to cover their basic needs". He also quickly went on to say that employees need to be "satisfied with the quality and meaning of their jobs", in addition to earning enough to cover their

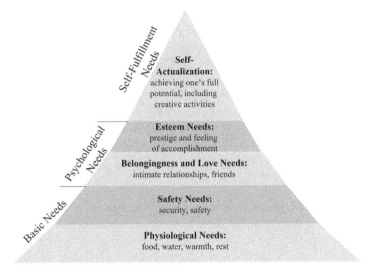

Figure 9.1 Maslow's Hierarchy of Needs.

Source: Adapted by the author from McDermid (1960).

needs. "Money is not always the only thing that matters", even in a low-income situation.

On the other hand, in Dubai, which is certainly not a typical emerging market, one executive pointed out that workers who had immigrated in from India or Pakistan were definitely concerned about meeting basic needs – for their families back home. Many or even most of these workers send a significant part of their compensation back to families in their home country, and keep what they need to pay for their housing, food and clothing in Dubai. They are not poor in a traditional sense of earning just enough to survive, but they in effect use the income above survival needs to support similar needs of their family members in another country.

Another executive in the Middle East, in the manufacturing conglomerate, said that:

> In our firm in the Middle East, we paid our employees a salary that was 30–40% below market rate but made sure the basic needs of the employees were taken care of. In some instances, we provided worker housing, internet, utilities, etc. While some of this housing was considered compensation, it still did not match the market rate. Everyone knew our company paid employees the least. However, we never, not once, lost an employee to a competitor; they became fiercely loyal to the company,

and we never suffered brain drain. When we posted job ads or went to a recruitment firm to hire, we could get the very best people applying for the position. Salary, I learned, was not the driving factor in the Middle East. Fulfilling basic needs, while not an intuitive part of the Western mindset, absolutely drives an Eastern (and in our case, a Middle Eastern) mindset and behaviors.

I also learned that when we provided for employee basic needs, the employee truly felt like the company cared about them because the company cared for them. Actions do speak louder than words. This enabled management to have difficult conversations about performance reviews or being able to hold employees accountable without the worry they will leave the company.

Even in the United States, basic needs have become more striking in the period just after the pandemic, as inflation soared, and people found it harder to meet their living expenses. A construction equipment executive said that: "We are very concerned that inflation is getting out of control, so we are giving raises twice a year. We help our people deal with these cost-of-living crises". This is much more fundamental than keeping up with the Joneses.

Are people working to maximize their incomes?

If we think about the United States or Europe or Japan, where basic needs are not usually the main concern of why people work, then what about the amount of work that people do? Do most people work 40 hours per week at a job in the marketplace (as opposed to home activities such as cooking, cleaning, raising children, etc.)? While it varies a bit between males and females, most people in the United States in early 2022 worked about 35 hours per week in jobs that pay income (Bureau of Labor Statistics 2022). This number has remained fairly stable for the past decade, excepting 2020 during the worst part of the Covid-19 pandemic.

With unemployment less than 4% for most of the last decade (excepting again 2020) in the United States, it does not seem that people are jumping at opportunities to increase their incomes by working more hours. There are certainly exceptions to this average, including hourly workers who often supplement their earnings with overtime or a second job. Still, the average person residing in the US works for about 35 hours per week, and so this does not appear to show that they are aiming to maximize their incomes.

An American executive who has worked in several non-profit organizations argued that: "Some people want money (income) for safety; some want more money for buying more stuff; some want money for their kids' education or other family needs/interests; some people go to work because they enjoy the camaraderie (social needs)". This is certainly not for maximizing income, although you can see that to pursue these goals a person may indeed want to work more hours to have more income.

This person also pointed out that: "The industry in question makes a big difference in what a person's needs are and what their social goals may be". For example, in a professional services context, or in a university, the professionals involved generally have no fixed work hours, other than occasional meetings with staff or clients (or students), and they also have the ability to work some or most of the time from any location they choose – from home, from an office, from a vacation place. These people will mostly accept their compensation levels and focus more on the quality of their work experience. In contrast, someone working in a repetitive process such as manufacturing or many consumer services, will have much greater interest in the salary level and the ability to spend time away from work. It really is not possible to generalize very far between such different kinds of work, other than to say that there are definitely non-income goals that people pursue in addition to their wages/salaries.

Just as in the United States, the Peruvian executive said that, for employees in his context: "Maybe their first goal is to satisfy their needs and to feel that they have a future in their job, but that is not always true when you are not satisfied with what you are doing. The quality of the job is very important". I interpret this to mean that, while employees are concerned about earning enough to pay the bills and to have a stable job, they still are looking for more than just income from the job. Non-monetary considerations are important, too – though it should not be ignored that the income earned from the job is vital as well.

Is the 'work/life balance' really an issue in your organization?

If people are not trying to maximize their incomes, then are they actively seeking to create a balance between work and other activities, the 'work–life balance'? My experience in banking, consulting and academe showed me that people generally do not look for a balance in their lives, but rather they work for income and satisfaction and then they either stick to hourly requirements if their work is paid hourly, or they work more than 'normal' hours if they are professionals or white-collar employees. They only look for 'balance' when they need to take a few hours off for a doctor's appointment for themselves or for a child, or for some other occasional issue at home, such as a repairman coming to fix the heater or the toilet.

And when it comes to taking vacations, people likewise tend to short themselves on vacation days, despite an employer's offer for such paid vacations. In the United States in 2018, workers took an average of 17.4 vacation days, while employers offered an average of 23.9 days of paid vacation that year. This adds up to 768 million days of unused paid vacation, of which 1/3 was simply lost to the employee. This does not seem like much of a work–life balance to me.

I have found that employees in my organizations have seldom talked about a work–life balance. Women may talk about taking time off for maternity leave, which is often paid leave from employers. But nobody has told me that he or she wanted to take more time off to pursue a hobby such as a sport (golf or tennis) or an art (painting or writing). And the people have backed up their lack of statements about taking leave to pursue other activities by not taking that leave!

The construction equipment executive said that his boss tells him to relax sometimes! The challenge of paying more attention to life outside of work starts at the top for sure. He adds that: "We do care about our employees' home lives, and that they are doing ok in that regard. The CEO knows a very large percentage of our more than 2000 employees, and he pays attention to them as people". This translates into offering people time off to deal with occasional family problems or crises and even financial support for unexpected costs (such as paying for added transportation costs of an employee whose job location was moved across town).

An executive in the oil and gas industry says that: "Work/life balance is a bit of a myth, because it dramatically ebbs and flows depending on a person's role and ambitions. In almost every role I have witnessed people fulfilling, a really critical project that has a hard deadline will require that work will need to get done with home life potentially squeezed as a result. I would argue people who are more motivated do work harder and with more initiative than others, so they can be compensated more. (And these people are also more inclined to jump jobs when they are not compensated for their perception of the value they are creating.)"

Due to the Covid-19 pandemic, many people have reconsidered their work activities, in some cases because of layoffs during the pandemic related to quarantines or lockdowns or other restrictions on business (e.g., on hotels and travel activities). If your employer could not provide you a work opportunity during this time, that certainly made you rethink your life and job. The pandemic itself made many people question their activities, work and otherwise, with the threat of possible infection and serious illness or death from the virus. This once-in-a-lifetime event has had a major impact on work, how it is done, where it is done, how many hours are spent and so forth. We are still observing and defining the 'new' world of work.

As many people post-Covid work part or all of the time from home, the definition of work–life balance is changing. Now that people don't have to spend time commuting to work on those days that they do not go to the office or other work location, they potentially have more time for their own non-work activities. Even so, we hear about burn-out of people who stay at home but cannot disconnect from email communications, Zoom calls, and other electronic interactions with work (e.g., Thomason 2021). They end up working more hours than before because of the constant feeling of a need to be 'on'. So, the work–life balance has to be re-calibrated to account for the greater commitment to electronic communications, and also the timing, which can often be during evenings and weekends.

According to the oil and gas executive,

> It has depended on the role, however most of the people who were traditionally working from an office like software engineers, electrical/ mechanical engineers, and other specialists have moved from the office environment to working from home (WFH). Higher skilled people have been able to continue working with the same productivity levels as they did in the office before Covid-19, if not higher. For sales and business development people who worked from home in 2019 and earlier, there has not been much of a shift.

So, this executive does not see much impact on a work/life balance due to Covid, other than the greater need to work from home.

Why do people work?

Once basic needs are accounted for, Maslow (1943) suggested a pyramid of higher-order human needs that people pursue, including belongingness, self-esteem and self-actualization. More recent efforts to look at this issue include the work by Deci and Ryan (2015), which they call Self-Determination Theory. This theory asserts that people have three psychological needs: for competence, autonomy and relatedness. People want the opportunity to develop and demonstrate their *competence*, for doing a job or in playing a game, or in other contexts as well. People want to have *autonomy* to do their jobs and manage their lives free of Big Brother or a boss telling them what to do. And people need to *relate* to other people, and feel that they are part of something bigger than they are as individuals. Everyone seeks these three kinds of goal to a greater or lesser degree in their work lives.

If we go back to the discussion in Chapter 2 about things that motivate people to work in an organization, we found that each of these elements appears. Demonstrated *competence* is something that generally produces praise from the boss, and praise is one of the fundamental elements of motivation discussed there. Recognition by not just the boss but from others in the organization also generally follows from demonstrated competence. And the opportunity to develop more competence is another of the features that we identified. *Autonomy* is valued today, perhaps more than in earlier times when more work was routine. The more that machines and software replace routine business activities, the more that people will want to have the freedom to carry out their work successfully without excessive oversight. So, autonomy continues to become more important in the workplace. And finally, the idea of *relating to other people*, both for the human interaction and also for feeling a sense of purpose in your work, is important. This issue was understated in Chapter 2, but there is no doubt that Deci and Ryan are correct that people want to have a sense of belonging in a social setting; they want to relate to other people.

There are certainly other conceptual views of the reasons that people work as well, though they are not discussed here (e.g., the Herzberg et al. 1959, two-factor theory of hygiene/motivation; McClelland's 1961, three-factor theory – achievement, affiliation or power). These other conceptual approaches attempt to identify more systematically those factors that motivate people to work, moving beyond the subsistence needs that they may have. Our interest is simply in recognizing that there are many more reasons for choosing to work, beyond paying the bills.

Did this change during and after the Covid-19 pandemic?

Covid-19 affected the work environment dramatically around the entire world, and there is no doubt that work life has changed in some ways for everyone. When people could not go to work due to lockdowns early in the pandemic, this caused many of them to consider changing their jobs. When the pandemic slowed down after more than a year, employers in many countries found that it was difficult to recruit adequate numbers of employees to fill their needs for many different kinds of jobs. In the United States over 100,000 unfilled jobs remained in 2022 in various service activities including cashiers, retail salespeople, waiters/waitresses and nurses (www.car eerprofiles.info/careers-new-openings.html). This has pushed employers to offer more attractive work environments, including higher wages, more job flexibility, and other perks.

The idea of greater job flexibility, or of higher wages, does not change the logic for why people work. It does perhaps make some jobs less attractive, when they are more constrained to a timetable, such as in working in a restaurant or on an assembly line. However, many jobs do not require that specific timetable or the direct interaction with customers or in operating a machine. For example, in professional services such as accounting, legal services, computer software design, and many others, timetables can be very flexible as can the location of work. So, these jobs have changed quite a bit with Covid-19, and people in these services still are working at least partially from home or at least not from the office, often with flexible hours as well. Some companies are even choosing to let people work a 32-hour week in four days, rather than the traditional five days and 40 hours, for the same pay (Willans and Lockhart 2021; Agovino 2020).

The Peruvian executive said that: "Yes, there is a change, I see more employers looking after their people, especially for companies that have been severely affected due to COVID-19. In many cases employers have not dismissed workers, and that has paid off". At the same time, "unemployment has forced some people to be creative and develop new types of business".

The results of the Covid-19 pandemic will be felt for many more years, even though the pandemic itself has retreated by late 2022 to a more common flu-like disease. The changes in working conditions that occurred due to the initial lockdowns and fear by people who did not want to congregate in workplaces has become part of the business world today. Many people work at least part of the time from home. Work hours have become somewhat more flexible. Doing business via Zoom or some other telecommunications medium has become standard fare for a large percentage of the population. As we see the pandemic diminishing, it is clear that work life has changed dramatically for some and significantly for most. People still have the need and various motivations to work, but the way that they do it has changed notably from the first part of the 21st century.

Work attitudes of millennials

One enormous change in work attitudes has occurred in the 21st century well before the Covid-19 pandemic. This is the arrival of the Millennials (people born 20 years before the new millennium, that is, in 1980, up to 2000) in the workforce starting in 2000. This group of people has demonstrated a clear commitment to life goals such as protecting the environment and treating people fairly, especially women and minorities. While these ideals were discussed long before the Millennium, most of us did not really pursue them with any major commitment. (I recognize that there are exceptions.) Today we see many university graduates choosing, for example, not to work for oil companies, because of the pollution and environmental damage caused by that industry – just as since the 1970s people generally chose not to work in the tobacco industry, because of the health damage that was demonstrated to occur from smoking.

And treating people fairly has likewise become much more serious in the era of the Millennials, as we see with worldwide protests by women for equal treatment and to stop sexual harassment, as well as anti-racist movements such as the Black Lives Matter (BLM) effort in the United States. These movements have caused major confrontations between protestors and police, as well as by opponents (e.g., the huge BLM protests on June 6, 2020, after the death of George Floyd two weeks earlier at the hands of police in Minneapolis). The issue of fairness is not new, and companies have been required by US law to offer fair treatment to people in hiring and compensation decisions for many years, even though enforcement is uneven and the definition of exactly what is fair sometimes is difficult to agree on. Even so, the issue has become much more prominent in business life in the 21st century than it was earlier.

Millennials also tend to view their work activities more vitally in the way they relate to the rest of the world, in the two contexts mentioned above of dealing with the environment and with fairness among people, as well as in terms of how much they want to work. Employers from restaurants and hotels to consulting and investment banking firms are discovering that their younger employees are not as willing to work herculean hours just to move up the career ladder, when other issues such as those above are relevant to their lives. These employees are demonstrating by their willingness to leave such jobs for alternatives when they feel overburdened are pretty different from their predecessors, who used to complain about such things but did not vote with their feet (i.e., leave employers for these reasons). Only a dinosaur of a boss would fail to pay attention to these changes in attitudes toward work among the Millennials.

According to the executive in the Middle East manufacturing conglomerate,

> Inherent in every individual is the desire to grow, progress and make a meaningful contribution to the world or their workplace. If the basic needs of an employee are covered and if employees feel like they are making a real contribution, they will give their souls to the firm. People want to work and do meaningful things; when they do, they feel joy and joy is a motivating feeling (but a word not often used in the work place).
>
> Sustainable Development Goals and/or the ESG (environmental, social, governance) movement is about doing the right thing and making a profit. Millennials and Gen Z'ers want to do more than make a salary, they want to make a difference. Making a meaningful difference for others brings joy and joy is what is lacking under traditional models of the corporation. When employees don't feel that higher satisfaction, they wonder if their time and contribution mean anything. If the only goal is to make more money, then at some point, the work feels meaningless. Being in an environment where one feels their contributions are meaningless is depressing and leads to greater anxiety; Millennials and Gen Z'ers avoid depression and anxiety at all costs these days!
>
> I have learned though that a company does not necessarily have to be explicit (although it helps) about their ESG goals. They simply need to pursue these goals in a meaningful way without hypocrisy or guile; employees are smart and will see if the company is sincere while seeking to do good. If they feel the company is "good", they will find greater meaning in doing their work.

This perspective has spilled over onto Gen Y and older employees as well, so that the workplace today is much more employee-friendly.

Do people around the world care about Sustainable Development Goals (SDGs)?

The United Nations developed a list of 17 Sustainable Development Goals (SDGs) back in 2015, after pursuing a shorter list of eight similar goals during 2000–15. Those previous goals, aimed mostly at reducing poverty, were called the Millennium Development Goals. They were substantially achieved – or at least major advances were made – so the 2015 goals are more ambitious and more wide-ranging. The original goals included targets such as eliminating extreme poverty, reducing child mortality, combatting HIV and malaria, and empowering women. Huge advances were achieved on almost all of them in 15 years. The new goals are listed in Figure 9.2, and they include eliminating poverty and hunger, improving education, protecting the environment, achieving sustained economic growth, and increasing equality around the world. The reason for talking about the SDGs here is that Millennials are paying attention to many of these goals, and employers need to respond to them in order to attract and keep Millennials in their organizations. The demonstration effect has also to some extent altered attitudes of previous generations who remain in the work force, and who today often want their organizations to pursue the SDGs as well.

And it is not just Millennials. People in countries around the world, Triad countries and emerging markets alike, are paying attention to some or many of these SDGs. Today companies have to respond to these concerns both to attract employees who embrace things like environmental protection and

Figure 9.2 UN Sustainable Development Goals.

(Reproduced from www.un.org/sustainabledevelopment. The content of this publication has not been approved by the United Nations and does not reflect the views of the United Nations or its officials or Member States).

better healthcare, as well as to avoid penalties that range from legislation that disallows polluting activities to social media protests against companies that fail to hold high standards for ethical behavior. This is a fascinating change from the business environment of the late 20th century, when these same issues were discussed, but very few people used them as criteria for choosing an employer or for pushing an employer to deal satisfactorily with them.

The SDGs include topics that definitely drive Millennials' thinking about employers, such as Goal #5 on Gender Equality, and Goal #13 on Climate Action. At the same time there are other SDGs that are narrower in their applicability, such as building sustainable cities (#11) or life below water (#14). So, the message is not that companies and other organizations need to embrace all of the development goals, but rather that they need to recognize that some people do feel strongly about many of them, and the employers need to make sure that they do respond to those issues that are found to motivate their employees.

Another label for these non-business goals that companies pursue today is 'ESG' (environment, social, governance). This label has developed parallel to the UN goals, and it seems to have replaced the idea of corporate social responsibility in company policy and public discussions. According to a McKinsey study in 2022, "More than 90 percent of S&P 500 companies now publish ESG reports in some form, as do approximately 70 percent of Russell 1000 companies". And corporate spending on ESG projects, especially related to the environment have risen dramatically:

> Inflows into sustainable funds, for example, rose from $5 billion in 2018 to more than $50 billion in 2020—and then to nearly $70 billion in 2021; these funds gained $87 billion of net new money in the first quarter of 2022, followed by $33 billion in the second quarter
>
> (Perez et al. 2022, p.1)

It does appear that companies and people generally, not just Millennials, are paying serious attention to these socially responsible activities today.

Conclusions

It is clear that people work both to earn enough income to meet basic needs and to pursue other goals ranging from self-realization to moving up in an organization. Basic needs are important, especially to people with low incomes in any country. However, even workers in unskilled or low-skill jobs do demonstrate a concern for the quality of their working conditions and for things such as respect from co-workers and a feeling that their work matters. It seems that once subsistence needs are met, people immediately shift their attention to the additional job characteristics, so employers need to focus their attention on much more than compensation.

Millennials and earlier generations who remain in the work force today are demanding more flexible work conditions, often including the ability to work from home some of the time. They also are concerned about social issues such as equality among people and protection of the environment. These formerly tangential issues have become mainstream in the workplace today, and employers need to focus on them as well as on operating efficiently and successfully.

References

Agovino, Theresa, 2020. "The phenomenon of the four-day workweek". www.shrm.org/hr-today/news/all-things-work/pages/four-day-workweek.aspx

Bureau of Labor Statistics, 2022. "Average weekly hours and overtime of all employees". www.bls.gov/news.release/empsit.t18.htm

Deci, Edward, and Richard Ryan, 2015. Self-Determination Theory. In James Wright (ed.), *International Encyclopedia of the Social & Behavioral Sciences*, 2nd ed., Amsterdam: Elsevier. Volume 21, 487–91.

Gallup, 2020. "Millions vulnerable in developing and developed world". May 20. https://news.gallup.com/poll/315851/millions-vulnerable-developing-developed-world.aspx

Herzberg, F. I., Mausner, B., and Snyderman, B., 1959. *The Motivation to Work*, 2nd ed. New York: John Wiley.

Maslow, Abraham H. (1943). A theory of human motivation. *Psychological Review*, 50(4), 370–96.

McClelland, David, 1961. *The Achieving Society*. Princeton, NJ: Van Nostrand.

McDermid, Charles, 1960. How money motivates men. *Business Horizons*, 3(4), 94.

Perez, Lucy, Vivian Hunt, Hamid Samandari, Robin Nuttall, and Krysta Biniek, 2022. "Does ESG really matter—and why?". *McKinsey Quarterly*. August.

Thomason, Bobbi, 2021. Help your team beat WFH burnout. *Harvard Business Review* online. January 26. https://hbr.org/2021/01/help-your-team-beat-wfh-burnout

Willans, Ashley, and Charlotte Lockhart, 2021. A guide to implementing the 4-day workweek. *Harvard Business Review*. https://hbr.org/2021/09/a-guide-to-implementing-the-4-day-workweek

Chapter 10

Conclusions

Introduction

The reason that I began writing this book was because I found that there were just too many occasions in my business and academic dealings around the world when people acted very similarly, no matter what language they spoke, the color of their skin, whether they were male or female, or what opinions they may have had. People love to talk about how different we are from each other, whether it be the languages we speak, political points of view or the meanings of gestures such as shaking hands or bowing or standing close or far from each other when talking. There is no doubt that these things are true, and that cultural differences do exist. But the basic humanity of us all needs to be emphasized as well.

Review of Findings

The discussion in the chapters above has focused on eight elements or dimensions along which people are quite similar around the world. They include:

1   Things that motivate people within an organization
2   Things that de-motivate people within an organization
3   How trust is important in business, and how trust can be built in an organization
4   How people have respect for each other and how the organization can foster that
5   How fairness is demonstrated in an organization and how to generate perceptions of fairness
6   How honesty and integrity are solid foundations for running an organization
7   How looking forward and planning are vital parts of running a successful business
8   What the reasons are that people choose to work.

DOI: 10.4324/9781003367512-10

Here are a few thoughts about each dimension.

1   **Motivations**. People are motivated by positive feedback from their supervisors and from other people in general. There are many additional aspects of a work environment that can motivate individuals to commit to their work, ranging from higher salaries/wages to greater perks such as vacation time, access to training/education opportunities and other things. People like to be recognized for doing good work, and they also like to have interesting, stimulating work to do. Even the idea of a stable work environment, without the threat of layoff, provides another form of motivation. And especially in the 21st century, people tend to like to think that their work is meaningful, rather than just being a source of income.

2   **De-motivations**. Of course, things that de-motivate people can just be the opposite of what motivates them. Negative feedback for weak performance without adequate effort to suggest ways to improve or otherwise to soften the blow of criticism is extremely de-motivating. Low compensation, few opportunities for training and an unstable work environment with a high risk of layoffs all produce the opposite reaction from the factors mentioned earlier as motivators. Additionally, a job that lacks a sense of purpose or importance will de-motivate people – even while the possibility may be right there for a supervisor to try to identify purpose for the employee, and coach the employee on the importance of the job. A fascinating challenge is to mete out praise and criticism fairly and explicitly to people, given that we know that criticism is de-motivating. If you try to treat everyone equally, and to avoid criticism, then those who see the poor performance of a co-worker will be de-motivated. And if everyone receives the same praise for their work, then those who perform better will be de-motivated. It is a difficult challenge for the boss!

3   **Trust**. It typically takes a while for people to feel trust for another person or for an organization. You want to see trustworthy behavior before placing your trust in someone. A boss or another employee can be seen as trustworthy if she routinely follows through on commitments to subordinates and colleagues. Being transparent in decision-making also can generate trust among employees. And giving people freedom to do their jobs without excessive supervision can build trust as well. An organization can demonstrate trustworthiness by not laying off people except in extreme circumstances (e.g., during Covid-19). It can provide information about criteria for promotions and raises, training opportunities and other benefits, and then by following its own guidelines it can be perceived as trustworthy.

4   **Respect**. People deserve respect as human beings, and any organization needs to ensure that this kind of respect is given. This is often called

'owed respect'. At the same time, people gain respect based on their performance of jobs or tasks, such as developing new products or dealing successfully with clients. Respect for this kind of performance can be called 'earned respect'. Both types are important in an organization – though there are even other kinds of respect as well. For example, respect for elders, or respect for someone in a high position within the organization are additional reasons for respecting the person's characteristics, rather than his/her behavior. And even self-respect should be included in the list, since it has been shown that greater self-respect can enable a person to perform better on the job.

5   **Fairness**. As with respect, there are several dimensions of fairness. A useful division looks at *process* or *procedural fairness*, in which decisions in an organization are made transparently and by applying the same rules to everyone. This contrasts with *outcome fairness*, which treats people in similar circumstances equally. People with similar performance should be rewarded similarly. And finally *approach fairness* calls for the organization to identify its goals and the performance that is consistent with those goals – and then to reward people for success in pursuing those goals. This is a bit more complicated, because the approach today generally requires companies to pursue both returns for shareholders and also outcomes that speak to issues such as social justice (racial and sex non-discrimination) and environmental   protection (reduction of carbon dioxide output). So, the multiple goals need to be incorporated into the performance evaluation of employees. All three of these aspects of fairness are important in company evaluations, and employees' *perceptions* of that fairness are probably more important than actual measures of fairness.

6   **Honesty and Integrity**. These are not the same thing. Honesty means acting in a truthful manner. Integrity means adherence to moral and ethical principles. A person could be honest, but be unethical. (For example, a person may treat others in a despicable manner, but still could be honest about it. Or in the extreme, you could kill someone, but still be honest and admit it.) A person with integrity should therefore be honest and also act according to morally sound principles. The issue of honesty in business is not black and white, because in order to run a company successfully, it may be important for an executive sometimes to paint a rosier picture than reality – in order to avoid a big stock price plunge that might follow an admission of short-term problems in the company (or a run on the bank in the case of a financial institution). While honesty and integrity are not guaranteed to produce better corporate performance, the focus today on issues such as corruption, and the widespread rejection and penalization of this practice, seem to signal that countries are paying attention to improving the integrity of business activities.

7 **Looking Forward.** I think we can agree that it is important for an organization to be forward-looking, if only to avoid crises that can be foreseen from simple observation of the business environment. For example, projecting how much inventory will be needed for next quarter, and then acting to make sure that it is obtained on time is clearly a valuable endeavor. But it is not at all clear as to how far forward an organization should be looking. An annual strategic planning process is probably a very good idea, since it forces the leaders of the organization to pay attention to issues that may come up in the year ahead, and it offers an opportunity to make decisions to deal with expected challenges and opportunities. But of course the actual detailed plan is less important than the process of putting it together and thinking about the future. People at any level of an organization can pay attention to figuring out ways to improve their productivity, including the observation of other similar organizations to see how they deal with the details of operating the business. We don't all have to be fortune tellers to know that we should be looking forward in managing our organizations. Managers can put forward-looking behavior into the key performance indicators used to reward people in the organization, so such thinking can be encouraged in this way.

8 **Reasons for Working.** This chapter was conceived as a discussion of how important income from working is to people. As I thought about it, and talked with executives about it, I realized that income is certainly important, but so also are other goals. And so the discussion looks at the various goals that people have from their work activities. The additional goals include enjoyment of the work, or satisfaction about the work. This can come from feeling that your work is important or makes a difference in the world, and/or that people appreciate what you are doing. Additional reasons for working are to achieve competence in what you do, and also to have sufficient freedom to do the work without a manager constantly hanging over your shoulder. In this chapter as well as in earlier ones, the discussion turns to how Millennials and Gen Z people look at their work, and whether they have different reasons from earlier generations. The one thing that sticks out consistently is that Millennials pay more attention to non-business goals, the so-called Environmental, Social and Governance (ESG) issues. People of all ages today are more involved with pursuing these goals, but it is only in the 21st century that ESG issues have come to the forefront.

In every case of these eight dimensions people around the world have very similar views, even if they may demonstrate their respect or their trust or their commitment somewhat differently in different contexts. Whatever the context, people are people.

The lessons for managers and executives are clear; you can motivate people, generate trust among employees, encourage a forward-looking organization, and generally accomplish goals along each of the dimensions by following the guidance offered by the analysis here. And you can benefit from the experience of executives from around the world as discussed under each of the dimensions.

Additional areas for executives and managers to consider for improving organizational performance

There are unquestionably other issues that can be explored to see how people are similar across countries and cultures and also how to build an organization to take advantage of those similarities. In recent years there has been a strong tendency for people in quite a few countries to identify themselves as different from others based on political outlook. This is vividly clear in the United States, with the Trump 'revolution' causing Democrats and Republicans to move further apart toward the left and right, respectively. How can an organization avoid being caught up in this political firestorm? I think that most people would agree that we will not see a convergence of viewpoints here, so that a company or other organization will probably be best served by minimizing the amount of discussion of political issues at the workplace. This is easy to say, but may be difficult to implement! Even so, the idea of trying to keep political lobbying out of the workplace, and to focus people's attention on other issues such as operating the business successfully and pursuing whatever other goals are agreed to be appropriate for the organization.

As I write this I realize that this is really a tall order. Allowing freedom of speech, and still avoiding (intense) discussions or arguments about politics is not an easy combination to achieve. Nevertheless, this is the kind of approach that will enable an organization to operate with people of both political views to coexist peacefully and hopefully harmoniously. The leaders of the organization probably cannot dictate what issues may be discussed at work, but they can look to themselves and the leadership team to demonstrate non-conflictive behavior on political themes, and try to encourage employees to do the same.

Another issue is *the question of where work is carried out – at home or at the office*. It seems that once again cultural differences are smaller than the similarities of conditions facing people around the world today. During the Covid-19 pandemic many types of businesses such as restaurants and hotels were forced to close to try to stop the spread of the virus. It did not matter if you worked in New York or Johannesburg or Tokyo, many businesses were forced to close for months at a time. As a result of this forced change in circumstances, many restaurants learned to provide delivery service for their meals. Hotels did not have such a capability, and so hotels globally suffered layoffs and prolonged work stoppages.

As a result of electronic communication through email and especially interactive video such as Zoom, people found that they could often work from home rather than from the office. The fact that this turned out to be fairly successful in getting work done has led to a post-pandemic continuation of working from home. Today the question is often: How many days per week do you have to actually go to the office? This question has not been answered in a definitive way thus far, although it does seem that some work will remain remote for a long time to come if not permanently.

So, how does this phenomenon of remote working play out around the world and across cultures? I observe that it is pretty similar in most places. If you work in a personal service such as haircutting or lawnmowing, you have to physically be there to provide the service. In other cases such as commercial banking, much of the human interaction had already been replaced by automatic tellers and electronic communication with the financial institution. This banking trend has just moved forward more rapidly to reduce the human interaction (although of course interaction does continue to occur through telephone and interactive video communications between banker and client.) In office work it appears that a substantial proportion of people are working a large part of the time from home. City centers that before 2020 were bustling with daily activity have declined dramatically, with many restaurants failing, retail stores failing, office buildings going unused, and other services also curtailed due to reduced customer traffic.

This global phenomenon of greater remote working and the resulting need to reshuffle the products and services sold in urban office concentrations is a major change in the way we work. It has produced a boom for services such as package delivery (e.g., Amazon and UPS), videoconferencing (e.g., Zoom, Microsoft Teams) and restaurant delivery at home (e.g., by the restaurants themselves or through Grubhub or UberEats). This is true around the world, although some of the main providers differ in different countries. The key point here is that we all are facing this changed world, and our responses are fairly similar across countries, although different in different industries.

Discussion of working remotely reminds us of the fact that this way of working was a direct result of the *Covid-19 pandemic*. This (hopefully) once-in-a-lifetime event really changed a lot in our world. Not the least of the changes was an opportunity for people to reflect on their lives and their work – and to decide if they wanted to continue on the path where they were. Of course, this opportunity was forced on those whose businesses were closed by shutdowns and quarantines, mostly in 2020, but continuing intermittently after that for more than another year. Many people changed jobs by force or by choice due to the pandemic.

One of the results of the business restrictions during Covid-19 was the recognition that supply chains (or global value chains) are risky if one point in the chain is cut off for an extended period of time. Then companies cannot rely on their suppliers, and products and services are delayed and otherwise disrupted. One lesson from this experience is that companies are building into their supply chains more than one source for key components and other inputs. Again, this is a phenomenon that is global, and all of our companies have to deal with the challenges of supply chain disruption.[1]

Another issue is the broad question of whether Millennials (born between 1980 and 1996) and Gen Z people (born between 1995 and 2015) are different from previous generations who are still in the workforce. To simplify the idea: Are Millennials different?

There is no doubt that Millennials are different in being more demanding that organizations pay greater attention to ESG issues such as environmental protection and equal rights for women and minorities. These issues are not new, but companies are now paying much, much more attention to them, rather than just focusing on being profitable and making shareholders happy. I would hazard a guess that older generations who remain in the workforce also are now paying more attention to these issues, so that Millennials are not alone in pursuing such goals.

At the same time, the Millennials are not that different from previous generations in many ways. One thing that really surprised me when looking at job-hunting activity of people in different age groups was how similar we are. In surveys done by the US Department of Labor since the 1960s, it turns out the people who were in the 25–34-year-old category stayed with their employer for an average of 3.0 years in early years; whereas in 2020 people in this category stayed with their current employer for 2.8 years – not much of a difference. Similarly, for people between 45 and 54 years old in 1983, they stayed with their current employer for an average of 9.5 years; in 2020 this group of people were with their current employer for an average of 7.5 years, a slightly greater decline than for the younger employees (all information from the Bureau of Labor Statistics).

I won't go further in pointing out phenomena and changes in the work environment that affect people around the world in fairly similar ways. We all face these challenges, male or female, old or young, English or Chinese speaker and so forth. We are all in the same boat, so to speak, and we all should be rowing together to make our lives more enjoyable and our work more meaningful. People are people.

Note

1 This supply chain risk was strikingly revisited with the Russian invasion of Ukraine in February of 2022. After that event, which has continued for many months, people around the world have encountered shortages of wheat and soybeans and other grains produced in Ukraine and Russia, as well as a huge increase in gasoline prices as Russian oil and gas are restricted by most countries. The challenge of making supply chains more resilient exists everywhere.

Index